"A well-written, witty, engaging, and ultimately informative book explores a growing question plaguing twenty-first century women: have we forfeited our connection to family and motherhood in the quest to 'have it all'? Taken from the perspective of a wanna-be grandmother who wonders if teaching her daughter feminist lessons left out part of the message—the happiness and satisfaction that comes from having children and a strong family life. Doctors, psychologists, mothers, and daughters are all given a voice in this well-researched, thought-provoking tome that explores the why, what, and how of making choices about having babies in today's world of new technology vs. our ancient biology."

— Dorothy Leeds, author of *The 7 Powers of Questions: Secrets to Successful Communication in Life and at Work*

"Debbie Slevin tackles head-on the discussions that need to take place with respect to the single and childless women of waning fertile years and to those married, but delaying pregnancy. Each chapter delves into the varying perspectives of professionals, religious leaders, women and men, as to how and why this "unpregnant pause" is occurring and why it is necessary to talk about this now. It's a book like no other regarding the insight of a woman's right to choose in contrast with the more often "unchoice" of childbearing. *UnPregnant Pause* delves deeply into society's failure to address that fertility and pregnancy are governed by biology and are in unresolved conflict with pressures for women during their peak fertile years to "lean into" their careers."

— Alice Meehan, Esq.

"This book is a warning to those that think 'this will not happen to me, I can have it all!' Fairy tales don't always come true, so while a career and personal interests take precedence in their lives, women should prepare alternatives for the day when they want to have a family and their 'time' has run out."

— Bassima Mustafa, New Jersey Educator

"Debbie Slevin offers an insightful and honest perspective on an important current and widespread topic. Carefully curated and well-researched, *UnPregnant Pause* deepens our understanding of a dilemma that many women (and men) face. Thought-provoking, relatable and thoroughly enjoyable, I recommend this book to friends, colleagues and patients alike. Anyone who wants to make an informed decision about whether to leave a stagnant relationship, when to have children, or how to prioritize career and parenthood NEEDS to read this!"

— Dr. Julia Yacoob, Clinical Psychologist

"Where have all the babies gone? Plagued by this phenomenon and a desire for grandchildren, Debbie Slevin journeys for answers through the minds of experts, family, friends and strangers. *UnPregnant Pause* is an informative, well-researched yet witty read that explores the impact of parenting and lifestyles throughout generations, and in doing so, incites meaningful discussions for book clubs of all ages and genders."

— Maris Sattely, Esq.

UnPregnant Pause

WHERE ARE THE BABIES?

UnPregnant Pause

WHERE ARE THE BABIES?

Dear Marisa –
Thanks for having me at NV –
Viva la "Cause"!
Debbie Sl[illegible]

Debbie Slevin

An imprint of Parables & Books
www.figlopress.com

Published by Figlo Press, an imprint of Parables & Books, LLC.

Printed in the United States of America
10 9 8 7 6 5 4 3 2 1
First Edition

Statistics presented herewith reflect data aggregated and maintained by credited national and private researchers accurate at time of publication. Inclusion was explicitly granted when required, otherwise protected by public records laws.

Library of Congress Cataloging-in-Publication Data
is available upon request.

ISBN: 978-1-939682-17-8

Visit us on the web!
www.figlopress.com

PUBLISHER'S NOTE
Figlo Press is committed to publishing works of quality and integrity. In that spirit, we are proud to offer this book to our readers; however the story, experiences and words are the author's and the interviewee's.

For Jeff
Thank you.

CONTENTS

FOREWORD

Lila E. Nachtigall, M.D.

As a physician dedicated to taking care of women, I certainly have seen cultural changes in my over 40 years of practice. However, the change that took place in 25 to 40-year-old women was subtle. It did seem that fewer of them were married, and certainly many more stayed childless, and they were older when they came for help with fertility (often too old!). Surprisingly, it didn't dawn on me that this was a true modification of lifestyle that was happening all over the United States. It took Debbie Slevin, calling me about writing this book, to open my eyes to a phenomenon happening right under my nose!

Slevin has not only noted it, she's living it through her daughter and her contemporaries. When she polls her book club, of the seven daughters among them in this age group, only one is married and she has not (yet) born a child. Debbie sets out to discover why this is occurring, if it is beneficial for anyone and if it can be fixed for those who need fixing.

I truly enjoyed the statistics included here. As a scientist, I like proof. The one that had the most "wow power" though was that in the 25-29 female age group: 12% of women were unmarried in 1970 compared to 48% unmarried in 2008!!

By interviewing men and women, physicians and psychologists, fertility specialists and philosophers, Slevin achieves an amazing understanding of the issues which should be read by all parents before and after their children reach adolescence, as well as by all post-adolescents before they make major life choices.

A very important aspect that appears in her interviews with both scientists and philosophers alike is that although we aim for true equality between men and women, it can never happen. Despite the achievements of the Women's Movement, men still get to comfortably combine work and family and to do most of the choosing of mates. I think we should accept that and take men as allies.

Comparing recent popular authors: Sandberg who says "lean in" and take over at work, and Patton who says find a guy early and assure yourself a home, Slevin comes to the conclusion that they both have important points to offer. Different elements of advice can be pulled from each work to suit the needs of a great variety of women.

I feel I was a good interviewee, as I was married in the 1950s, succeeded in becoming a physician, never missed a day of work and brought up three successful daughters. But as I told my story, it was clear that I was looked down upon by many of the other mothers at school for not being home for my daughters, and it became clear to both Debbie and me that in the last 25 years, that message has often turned around and now the shame is on a woman for not having a career. The message clearly should be, as you will surmise when reading these pages, that there are many individual lifestyles, and liberating women means allowing them to choose lifestyles that work for them. It is not a disgrace to be a housewife and enjoy it any more than it is not a problem to select work dedication with or without a partner and with or without children. “Having it all” has a different definition for each of us, and this is the communication that UnPregnant Pause so strongly imparts.

PROLOGUE

"Mom, get up! You're making a spectacle of yourself," says my 32-year-old daughter. I am kneeling on the floor of Bloomingdale's playing peek-a-boo with a soggy blanket and the chubby-cheeked baby in the stroller behind us at the sales counter.

"I want one of those!" I whine plaintively.

"That's nice," she says. "Adopt." Everyone within earshot laughs. She's clever, I think. Smart. Funny. Accomplished. Financially independent. *Single.*

I am 59 years old and I want to be a grandmother. Before it's too late. Before I am sitting in the assisted living facility (don't call it a "home" because it's *not*). I am desperately afraid that I will miss that specific window of time when grandma bakes chocolate chip cookies with the tots and brings them sugary treats their parents say they can't have.

I have counted on this. Planned for it. I have kept every sticky finger-printed, broken-spined classic children's book on my basement bookshelf. I have the Tinkertoys and the really expensive wooden blocks from F.A.O. Schwartz. And *all* the Legos. Oh my—*boxes* and *boxes* of Legos. And a tissue paper-wrapped woolen blanket from each of my babies' infancy that comes with a matching story of where it was made and who gifted it (Grandma/Grandpa brought a pastel weave from Israel, long-lost friend Mandy chose a red woolen plaid from B. Altman's and my oldest friend Connie toted a fluffy mohair number all the way from Edinburgh.) All saved for my grandchildren.

I had my babies early with the expectation that I would be 52 when the youngest left for college and I would have all those still healthy (God willing!) years to be an active, involved grandparent. I imagined all the time I would have with my grandbabies for a stroll in the park or a cuddle as we read *Curious George* and *Corduroy* while my daughter and daughters-in-law take some precious time off for a pedicure, a massage, lunch with a girlfriend, work. I saw myself on the bleachers cheering at soccer games and in the auditorium at school concerts. I didn't plan to be just an observer, but an active participant. We would go skating, sledding and swimming together. I would sew costumes for Halloween and school plays. I could teach my grandchildren to dive and to plant. I was besotted by the perceived benefits of being a young grandparent. We would do 5K fundraisers together and hike in the woods.

"That's lovely," my daughter says. "Get a puppy." (*I did*)

But where *are* my grandchildren? Keen to my own yearnings, my ears have become attuned to this refrain. I hear it in the day-to-day conversation of women of my generation. In Starbucks, at work, at the grocery store, the nail place, book group, the subway. Wherever women my age congregate, they talk about their children, their unmarried, unpregnant, in their late twenties, mid-thirties and early forties children; especially the daughters who are trapped in the "UnPregnant Pause." And they bemoan their empty nests and empty arms.

I hear this chorus across the aisle and around the block. Over the river and through the woods . . . but not to grandmother's house. No one is coming to grandmother's house.

We are meeting our adult children in trendy restaurants or at the mall to buy couches for their apartments or suits for job interviews. And often, we are picking up the tab, treating them to something special, *mothering* them, harnessing and redirecting our maternal instinct by infantilizing our adult offspring ("Mom, e-NOUGH already," my youngest son says, holding up a flat palm. *The hand.*) But I've got nowhere else to put it. Either I fuss over them or the dog gets another chew toy. I *desperately* need a grandchild.

This is a serious question that begs examining, with a particular focus on our daughters: have we, the daughters of feminism (no, not the dirty word that feminism has been twisted into by radical political and linguistic manipulation, but the *second wave* feminism of the late '60s, the feminism of body-ownership and reproductive sovereignty), raised a generation that has so embraced the rights we fought for that our daughters' subsequent choices are not in sync with our expectations? Has the ownership of women's bodies—their reproductive freedom—and their entitlement to equal passage in society, defined by the right to choose career over family, the right to marry (or not) and quite possibly vastly different *criteria* for a spouse spawned a massive movement toward independence that results in a lack of coupling? Is this the flagrant banner of the success of our bra-burning liberation? My question, ladies, is this: have we done such a splendid job of helping our daughters become independent women that we are now reaping what we've sown?

I remember the moment like it was yesterday (and I admit I don't always remember yesterday so well): I was shopping with my daughter and she was eyeballing a very beautiful item of clothing. She was in middle school and already very much her own person, not at all swayed by the trends and labels that the other girls were wearing. (No *Juicy* logos printed on the tush of *her* sweatpants.) It was simply designed, a beautifully knit cashmere sweater. Turquoise. She held the fabric between her fingers and rubbed it. Then she brought it up to her cheek and caressed her own face. I looked at the price tag and made an unattractive gagging noise. "But its soooo soft," she said.

"That's nice," I replied. "So's a polar bear. But neither one is coming home with us today. But I do have to admit, you've got good taste. You had better marry a rich man." The minute the words were out of my mouth I heard the echo of my mother's voice and I regretted it. Bad Message! Bad Mother! (Both of us.)

"Wait!" I said. "I'm sorry. I'm *wrong*. You don't need to marry a rich man; you need to get a good job. That way, you can fill your closet with as much cashmere as you want. Don't be dependent on a husband to fulfill your needs," I ran off at the mouth. "You want something? Work hard, earn your own money, and go out and get it for yourself."

And I believe that was the beginning. The beginning of teaching her that she could achieve her goals independently. Self-reliance. It does *not* take two to tango—well maybe to tango—but not to *dance*. Mary Tyler Moore sang it: "You're gonna make it after all!" Burger King touted it: "Have it your way!" And they weren't just talking hamburgers. Even motherhood could be achieved without a corporeal partner. "You've come a long way, baby!"

BABY?? What baby?!? Where? When I remembered this story and thereafter indulged in many years of self-flagellation, I decided to reach out beyond the cursory sampling of my immediate community to discover if, indeed, this is a generational phenomenon.

This book looks at the numbers and the women behind those numbers, both mothers and daughters. I talk to the experts and explore recent studies and census reports that indicate a dramatic rise in maternal age and point to longer time spent in the academic arena and workforce. I argue with "Princeton Mom" Susan Patton, author of *Marry Smart: Advice for Finding THE ONE,* who advises women to snag a husband in college when the pool is full, and I question Facebook COO Sheryl Sandburg, who has plastered the upscale women's business world with "can-do-it-all" cheerleading in her best-seller *Lean In: Women, Work, and the Will to Lead* to the point that the phrase "lean in" is now part of current vernacular. I want to understand what has driven droves of women with deep pockets (and some with deep credit lines) to fertility clinics by themselves. Something radical has happened.

But what? And why? Were different values transmitted from mother to daughter? Has our culture, the Women's Movement, and a singular middle-aged woman's experience as a wife and mother (*mine*), colored the message passed on? I have interviewed professionals and common folk. Mothers and daughters. Even some men. And while doing this, I am hoping my married son and his wife will do me the great honor of growing me a grandchild. Before I hit the assisted living *facility*. Which, by the way, there is nothing facile about it.

But first: the parameters. I started this project with the ladies I know: mothers and daughters, friends and cousins and branched out from there. They connected me with their friends, and friends of their friends. Sisters of the friends of friends. Roommates, colleagues, castmates, baristas and babysitters.

People asked about the project and said they knew someone who might be willing to talk to me. I searched for women outside my demographic, my community and my comfort zone. I pushed to find women from different backgrounds, both familial and ethnic. All in all, I sent questionnaires to almost a hundred women and followed up with about 50 daughters and 20 mothers. Some I interviewed over lunch with a side of tears. A few over coffee, bitter with anger. Others on the phone, offering a modicum of privacy to hide their emotions. I listened and typed and often asked them to repeat themselves so I might quote them accurately. Once I developed trust in the digital tape recorder I purchased, I started to record the conversations. It allowed me to be more present, more involved in our conversations.

I found most of the professionals through networking, a few I tracked down online. I met my first fertility specialist through a friend. He was so taken with the notion of examining this issue that he gave me a list of other doctors to contact. *And so on and so forth.* One generous doctor after another agreed to be interviewed and suggested I speak to their colleagues, every conversation adding another piece to this puzzling trend. Each of the experts allowed me to directly use their name and position, unless otherwise noted.

The women who agreed to be interviewed for this book did so on the condition of anonymity. With the guarantee that their privacy would be protected, they opened up to me in ways both raw and profound. I have used aliases for all their profiles and changed identifying details including careers and cities of residence. I have promised to honor their confidences and guard their vulnerability. And I will.

And the men? The dads wanted anonymity as well as the dating men. They did not wish to be judged in a court of public opinion for their views. Only those for whom the dating world is a source of income were willing to use their names. For them, any publicity is a good thing.

ONE

Our Mothers, Ourselves

"Where is my Virginia?" I asked my mother.

"Your *what*?"

"My Virginia. Donna Dunlap said I had a funny Virginia."

"And what were you doing when she said that?"

"Changing for swim instruction. In the cabin," said my maybe-six-year-old self.

"*Ooooh!*" said my mother, the former obstetrical delivery room nurse. "Donna Dunlap is a stupid girl. Or her mother is."

"But I don't want a funny Virginia!" I sobbed, feeling very bad about myself, but not exactly sure why. "What *is* a Virginia?"

"Vagina, sweetie. Vagina."

"Vagina?" I asked and looked down at my crotch. "It's for pee. And babies. How is it funny?"

I learned where babies came from at a tender age because "my mother the nurse" believed in the scientific approach when it came to body parts and their functions. This did not endear us to the other mothers with whom we carpooled to school. There were a number of phone calls complaining about my sharing knowledge with other children. "How *dare* your daughter tell my daughter how babies are made?"

There was no *peepee* and *weewee* in our house. Our genitals weren't given pet names or silly euphemisms. My brothers and

I were raised with real names for bodily functions. Urine came out of an opening in my vagina; later blood would come out of a different opening there, which were both separate from that other opening, my anus. That funny pouch around my baby brother's penis was his scrotum. We described our bowel movements with precision. "It was a hard BM" or it was a loose BM." I didn't know about "doody" until I was out in the world and realized I didn't use the same elimination-speak as my friends. I discovered I was missing out on a whole world of creative language. *Shiiiiit!*

In senior year of high school, I had the shocking realization that I was taking my base of correct information for granted. This was *not* how other families shared. One day during lunch module, one of my "besties" pulled me aside in the cafeteria. Her lower lip was trembling and she was fighting tears.

"Mary-Margaret, what's the matter?"

She leaned forward and whispered in my ear: "I think I am pregnant."

"Are you sure? Come with me."

I took her hand and hustled her off to the girls' bathroom at the back of Corridor D by the chemistry labs. It was a safe bet no one would take the long walk there to urinate or change a tampon if they were menstruating. (I didn't know what it meant to "have your friend" until high school.)

"What makes you think you are pregnant?" I asked. "When was your last period?"

"Last week."

"Then why do you think you are pregnant?"

"He touched me *there* with his finger and it had . . . you know, stuff on it."

"Did he go inside you?"

"NO!" she was horrified. I wondered where she had been during the sex education class in middle school. Maybe she was one of the girls whose mothers would not sign the permission slip for that girls-only class where they showed a film in the back of the gym, windows covered over with black construction paper.

"I really doubt you're pregnant," I said. "But if you want, I can check with my mom. But I am pretty sure that sperm on a fingertip outside the vulva can't make you pregnant."

"The *what?*" Mary-Margaret asked.

My mother was working full-time in a public high school as the health and sex education teacher at that point. By proxy, I thought I was pretty smart about this stuff. I had helped her make a display board of condoms and diaphragms for her senior class. There were colored condoms and ribbed condoms and French ticklers *(look it up)*. It took us *forever* and a whole tube of glue to make the diaphragm case stick to the poster board. It's relevant to add that although I was 18 and had a long-term boyfriend, we were not yet having intercourse. It was not *applicable* knowledge at the time, if you get my drift, and having had a difficult father, I was a bit afraid of men.

I brought my copy of *Our Bodies, Ourselves* (which was considered quite radical when it was first published in 1970) to school the next day in a brown paper grocery bag and gave it to Mary-Margaret. She stuffed it inside her backpack, went off to college to become a history professor, eventually got married and brought up two accomplished children. She has yet to become a grandmother, but when she does, she will know *exactly* how that happened.

Although my mother armed me with information, she also filled me with dread. Is this what marriage was? Trapped in a cycle of violence and abuse (she gave as good as she got) she and her numerous therapists devised a plan. She took what credits she could apply from her nursing license and went back to school for a teaching degree. (She went back again to get her master's degree at the age of 60. No fool this woman—she wanted to retire on the highest step of the teachers' pension.)

She took a full-time position when my older brother went to high school and I was in seventh grade, with my younger brother still in elementary school. She knew that work—financial independence—was the only way out of her marriage, aside from the two suicide attempts with the plethora of prescription drugs she received from the family doctor.

It wasn't difficult for her to go back to work, she had live-in help. *Moi.* At 12, I dusted. I ironed. I knew how to sort laundry and run the washer. I was pretty swift with a vacuum cleaner and I made a pretty mean meatloaf for a middle schooler. Oh *yeah*, every once in a while, I did my homework. But rather than encourage me to seek out a career that would suit my less domestic talents (I *did* win a writing competition in fifth grade), she inadvertently instilled in me only one specific desire: to get out of the house. College was the ticket. "Remember," she would drill into me during the application process, "get a teaching degree so you have something to fall back on." She just assumed I would fail. And fall.

I got out as soon as I possibly could, with a dual BS in Early Childhood Education and Human Development. It was a breeze, since I already had tons of hands-on practical experience. I wrote my senior thesis for Critical Issues in Family Development about my own screwed up childhood.

The professor hinted that he believed I had fabricated the family, as the climate in the home seemed unrealistic. "It couldn't have been *that* bad!" A narrow-minded man with no imagination.

I married six months after graduation at the ripe old age of twenty-two. I had seven jobs in four years and then was swallowed up by motherhood the way the whale ate Jonah. I had my babies pretty quickly. Four in seven years, the second stillborn at the end of term. (I probably would have kept on having babies in an attempt to "fix" things if I hadn't insisted the doctor double-knot my tubes on the last C-section.) I was in a big hurry to be the housewife extraordinaire. I figured I could avoid the career dilemma by postponing it . . . *oh, about 20 years*. I remember doing the math out loud. "If I have my first baby at 26, and the last one before 35, then I will be 52 when the little one goes to college. *Plenty* of time to develop a career. And then . . . grandchildren. Ah, the stupidity of youth and an incredible lack of quality parental guidance.

But what I learned during those long nights watching exercise infomercials while nursing sick babies and/or folding laundry (do you have any idea how many socks five people can use in three days? Do the math) was that I could change things going forward. The key was education. For myself and my daughter.

I was a mommy, yes. But wasn't I *more*? I read books, women's magazines, feminist tomes, took adult education classes, saw movies about liberated women and watched my classmates who chose different paths become lawyers and judges. Bankers and pediatricians. English professors and fashion executives. And while I drove carpool, taught drama in the afterschool enrichment program for kids of working mothers, wrote for a small weekly newspaper and worked in my garden, I talked. And talked. And I made sure that my girl, the oldest of my three kids, would know she had choices. Real choices. Not just in careers, but in life. She didn't need to be rescued. She could rescue herself.

I wanted her to know that she should never be hit. That she could control her own money. She could live alone. Travel by herself. Buy a puppy. That she *owned* her body and no one had the right to it without her permission. I wanted to empower her to say no to others and yes to herself. She was going to carve out her own future, not just run away into an early marriage, dodging fists and frying pans, like her mother. Somewhere during her high school years, I ceremoniously gave her the newest reprint of *Our Bodies, Ourselves* (bully for me).

I believe knowledge is power. For me and many women of my generation and socio-economic strata, *Our Bodies, Ourselves* was the Bible. It triggered a movement. One might even be so hyperbolic to say a religion: the belief in women as equal human beings in the Homo sapiens equation. In the beginning: there is YOU. Separate and different from Man. It is *your* body. Learn about it. Take care of it. *Protect* it. Get a mirror and *look* at it! Maximize its productivity. You have control.

Some women were empowered (bully for *them*). But for me, the knowledge was theoretical. I was missing the most (statistically) important ingredient: a champion to encourage me to pursue an independent path, and the courage to follow it. I sold out for security. But with an understanding and supportive husband and strong female role models that I consciously sought out in adulthood, I started to figure it out.

With the book entrenched in my psyche, it informed me in the deepest way, shaping my opinions. As a writer and teacher, it helped me embolden the next generation. As a mother, it shaped how I have raised my daughter and two sons. But the question I am asking myself now is: has all this empowerment come full circle and sunk its cold barren teeth into my still somewhat firm pilated ass? Has this independence gone so far as to create a singularity that a man cannot breech?

I want to know, and since I would never be so bold as to assume that my experience or my hypothesis is indicative of the greater experience of my generation, I decide it is time for some field research. I take out my metaphorical compass, stop for a Starbucks vente iced tea with two pumps Classic, and I am off on my quest. I am hopeful that my interviews with other women will prove me right. I like to be right. Who doesn't?

WHAT MY MAMA SAID

Judy has two daughters three years apart. She and her husband have given them a traditional Jewish upbringing in a suburb of New York City. At 53, Judy holds an undergraduate degree in finance and a master's degree in teaching. She works full-time in an elementary school. Both girls are out of the house, and she and her husband are financially secure enough to be enjoying this time of their life. They eat out, vacation and spend time as a family.

"My parents married late," she says. "My mother lived her life fully before becoming a mother and told lots of stories about her dating life before meeting my dad. My perception [was] that although she wanted to marry and have a family, her 'important' years were prior." Saddled with the responsibility of a divorced mother and an ill sibling, Judy says her mother was "unfulfilled." She worked outside the home to contribute to the family's income, but also for personal enrichment, as she loved her job at the very first big home and bath store. "She had an infatuation with the industry," Judy remembers. Linens as a path to career contentment, no better or worse than fashion or finance today; it was one of the few "acceptable" fields for women then.

Although her mother "led by example: her husband and kids came first in her life," Judy believed that when her own turn came to make choices for herself, she would lead an "exciting cosmopolitan life in New York City." An apartment, a glamorous job, interesting places: a different world! She was not going to be tied down to a traditional life.

The reality is that Judy married at 23 and never left the suburbs. But her daughters did. They both live and work in New York City. They have drinks at wine bars and downtown clubs, jog along the river, work at creative jobs for high profile companies. And at 25 and 28, neither is in a serious relationship. "I want my daughters to be loved and to love someone nice," she says. "I want them to become mothers so that I can be a grandma. And because I think they would be good moms."

Judy's own wish fulfillment is already at work. Her daughters are living the life she dreamed for herself. She takes great pride in their accomplishments and derives vicarious pleasure from their activities. They are independent career women in one of the most exciting cities in the world. But they are not working on the other piece: the piece that might insure a grandchild. Did they not get *that* message from their mother? Judy would like it to happen, but I am not sure that information was imparted with the same verve. It is not a progressive value, certainly not one that is considered enlightened in today's society. It might even carry the risk of being called "old fashioned."

Judy's daughters are not currently dating, although they do meet eligible men. They socialize in groups as do many of the young singles in New York City. And they are close to each other and their parents. Very close. The nuclear unit remains intact. Even though the girls no longer live with their parents, in this age of cell phones, they speak daily with their mother and the intimate sharing of lives continues. Does it leave room for a "significant other?" (Parents As Significant Other: *stay tuned.*)

Sally is 63 and has lived in an upper middle class region of New Jersey her whole life. She is divorced and supports herself by working full-time. "My mother was not a very verbal person," she tells me. "She had difficulty relating to people on an intimate level. I think this was because she never had an intimate relationship with my father. She taught by doing rather than saying." And what she taught Sally was "not to depend on any man for your happiness. She was fiercely independent."

With Sally's grandfather out of work due to depression, Sally's mother supported her family from the age of 18 by bookkeeping. "She was the breadwinner" because she had marketable skills. "I think in a certain way she resented this, and that is what formulated her opinion of men. She continued to work once she married my father," Sally says, "because her career gave her the confidence, appreciation and compensation she wasn't getting from her marriage. She also loved to spend money!" She would often buy five pairs of shoes at a time, knowing she could not do that on her husband's salary (Now *that's* freedom!)

Growing up, Sally had different goals. Career was secondary to family. "I knew that I wanted a family and I wanted to be married . . . I was always very creative so I imagined as an adult I would be able to pursue some sort of artistic endeavor, while placing my family first. This is *somewhat* what happened," she says, as she now works full time in an administrative position, but makes extra money with her artwork.

Sally has two grown children: a son who is married and has one child (a grandchild!!) and a daughter, 30, who lives in New York City. She is single and has a successful career that includes travel to interesting places and attending exciting commercial events. She has never had a long-term relationship.

"I came from a home where my mother worked and was not there for me a great deal of the time," Sally says. "I was fortunate that I was able to be home with my children in the early years and this was very important to me. My daughter, on the other hand, came from a family where her mother was very present, but she was exposed to a grandmother and [never married] aunt who were both very independent, career-minded women. So she clearly saw both sides of the coin from the dominant female figures in her life. I think this gave her the ability to see that both lifestyles can work and helped her determine what would make her happy."

Sally does not dwell on the fact that she divorced shortly after her daughter finished college and received no settlement. She is self-supporting and often struggles to accomplish her financial goals, a fact that does not go unnoticed by her daughter, who earns a higher salary. At a point in her life where she might have retired with a husband and perhaps his pension, she works long hours with limited vacation time available to enjoy the family that was her ultimate goal. The underlying message from independent mother to divorced daughter to single granddaughter: make sure you can earn a living first.

Proud and impressed by her daughter's success, Sally would still like her to experience motherhood. "I always wanted a huge, loving family . . . and although my daughter is career-oriented, I think having a child is a priority for her. I think there is no greater bond between a mother and her daughter than to participate together in the caring for a child/grandchild," she says.

Barbara is 64. She grew up in Tulsa, Oklahoma, the third of five children with a Latina mother and Pennsylvania Dutch father. Although her mother never said much about raising a family, "I just observed that it didn't look like much fun," says Barbara. "With five children all within a few years of one another, she was pretty busy . . . it wasn't an easy gig." She remembers a news flash coming across the black and white television screen while her mother was ironing. "Marilyn Monroe has been hospitalized for exhaustion.

"What's exhaustion mean?" she asked.

"Don't worry, you'll never get it. Only rich women go to the hospital for exhaustion. You'll work hard just like me and you won't have anything to do with exhaustion and hospitals."

Barbara had her first child at 21 and the second at 24. "I went into motherhood knowing it was mostly a lot of hard work and I never expected anything else. I would work for a living as my mother did."

"I frankly never wanted children. After seeing how gruesome it was to be a working middle class married woman, motherhood just looked like a black hole of sacrifice. A total drag." Barbara was interested in so much more: writing, travel, politics.

A single mother after three years of marriage, Barbara is now an accomplished journalist. She is proud of being "my own personal authority in my life. I ask no one permission to be who I am and to feel whatever I feel and do whatever I do." It is "wholly unimportant for me that my daughter become a mother, ONLY if she wants to be a mother, then I will take a stand for her desire and support her. I believe she can do anything she puts her mind to doing and I do believe she would like to be a mother."

Barbara's daughter Melanie says her mother let her know that having a family was "hard . . . rewarding, but still hard. It stifles your life." She urged her not to get married too early: "to wait, to wait, to wait." At 39, Melanie has had several long-term relationships, including a brief marriage. "I didn't want a traditional family because I had never seen a model of a happy one. It all looked horrible to me." But her thinking has changed. "I'm frightened of spending my life alone without a partner, without intimacy, without intellectual understanding and tenderness."

***

I ask myself this question over and over: What part has our mothers' unhappiness played in the lives of the daughters of women like Sally, Judy, Barbara and me?

Did the Women's Movement and feminism offer a map to independence that had us inadvertently steer our daughters away from the road to marriage and family? Did our own desire for a different life influence the messages we imparted or were we simply trying to protect *them* from either the unhappy marriages we saw growing up or found ourselves in?

I am sure there are many women who have had happy mothers and happy marriages themselves and whose daughters are still caught in the unpregnant pause. But I am sorry to report that for the most part, I did not find many when I put out my questionnaires. That may simply be a matter of who I was referred to and not a representational sampling reflective of the generation as a whole. I would like to say that is the case, although I don't believe it to be.

I used to think that my personal experience was atypical, that the war zone that served as our family home was unique. Didn't everyone else live at Beaver's house? Weren't the other homes on our tree-lined suburban street on the East Hill just like The Donna Reed show?

I know these television references are lost on anyone under 40 . . . wait, maybe 30 (*thank you, Nickelodeon!*), but it wasn't until much later in life, at high school and college reunions, that I discovered how many of those other homes were as dysfunctional as ours; that these shows were a wish fulfillment fantasy for the post-war baby boomers. And this dysfunction, this *thing* that defined my formative years, has been the driving force behind the family I have created. It became my first career goal—to do it right. To build a happier and healthier family. Having witnessed the physical and emotional abuse of my initially unempowered mother, and having read *the book*, it's no wonder I felt the need to arm my daughter with adequate protection to help create an impenetrable shield against any overtly dominating intimacy.

Our Bodies, Ourselves opened up new pathways and personal vistas. (*Look! That's my clitoris!*) Did that knowledge give us the burst of courage to change how we were raising our daughters? *Yes*. Did it empower some of us to lead the political charge for equal rights? *Not me*. Or for some, was it a way to integrate this new climate of liberation into the existing social structure? (Hey! Hey! Equal Pay! And *yes*, I will make cookies for the bake sale, chair the fall fundraiser and put a home-cooked meal on the table for dinner!) *Me*. Did we somehow convey the idea that our young women can do it all without the help of a man? *Maybe. Maybe.*

As Sally says, she was taught at an early age not to depend on a man for her happiness. Now her daughter follows in the footsteps of an independent grandmother, an accomplished single and childless aunt and a self-supporting single mother. She, too, is a successful, single workingwoman.

Judy knew her mother was unfulfilled, as was her own dream of an exciting cosmopolitan life, but her daughters are living exactly the life she imagined for herself. And now she gets to be a part of it. She meets them for drinks, theater, shopping. She *is* one of the girls and is manifesting her dream, a generation removed. And her girls are the very picture of accomplished single women embracing the big city.

Barbara has carried forward her own mother's message that motherhood and family life is really hard. She has done a good job of imparting that to her daughter, Melanie. Yet for all her indoctrination and independent career success, Melanie still longs for some of the benefits of a traditional relationship.

We are so proud of our girls! They have accomplished so much. They are bold and beautiful, independent and self-sustaining. But our hearts ache for them every night as they go to sleep alone.

TWO

The Reading Room

My parents may not have personally introduced me to all the choices brought forth by the feminist movement, but they *were* smart enough to buy a house in an outstanding school district. And what I learned there was how to research.

"Here's the hypothesis," English teacher John D'Ambra said. "Now prove or disprove." Use books. Use magazines. Look at that ridiculous little microfiche in the library (anyone under 40: please see Wikipedia), but remember to show sources and cite material. Craft your position based on real information.

He was the teacher who had the most profound effect on me. Mandy and I visited him in his home when he and his wife had their first baby. We were still in high school, both products of dysfunctional homes, yet models of domesticity. While our divorced mothers were out earning a living and socializing afterwards, we were home cooking pot roasts for our siblings and learning to knit. We discussed recipes and laundry detergents while stretching the long cords of our telephones from the kitchen wall to the ironing board. When we should have been preoccupied with adolescent yearnings, we were parroting the housewives we saw on television.

When our teacher's new baby was old enough for company, we were excited by the very adult idea of making a "new baby" visit. We crocheted a hat and booties and tucked them into layers of tissue paper in a pretty box tied with ribbon. We bought a box of cookies from the bakery and drove three towns over. We craved the normalcy of this young teacher and his pretty wife and their new baby. For one afternoon, we pretended to be grownups in a happy home.

I wrote to Dr. D'Ambra when I was in college, when I was trying to figure out who I was and what it all meant through the haze of pot I was smoking, the profound poetry I was writing, and the adolescent bullshit I was flinging: the "Meaning of the Universe" sprinkled with quotes from "Desiderata" *(Go placidly amid the noise and haste)*. It was my desperate and misguided attempt to find peace during the violent skirmishes that still erupted at home between my parents. He wrote back and asked if I knew what a Renaissance man was. I did not, nor did I even wonder then if there was a Renaissance *woman*.

But his question made me *ask* questions. Better questions than "Why was I born to these crazy parents?" He encouraged me to get outside myself. "Read," he advised. "Read everything. Take all the courses you are interested in. It's the only time in life when you are completely free to explore. Read. Read. READ! Expand your horizons," was his challenge.

"Fall back on . . . fall back on . . . fall back on," my mother whispered. "Be prepared for failure" was her message. Be safe.

"Open yourself to the world," D'Ambra wrote. It was so enticing, so exciting, but I was too afraid, stymied as much by fear of success as fear of failure. I wasn't supposed to succeed. No one had even told me I was even supposed to *try*.

I read in the paper not too long ago that D'Ambra died at the age of 63. He and the pretty wife had divorced and he married another teacher from school who died of cancer. I was surprised to discover his life was real in the same way everyone else's was. He had lived on an elevated plane in my consciousness for many years. But I have learned that pain and tragedy are the companions of daily living and no one is immune.

I have thought a lot about him as I undertook this project. "Read," he had written to me in my little dorm room. "Read." And so I have. I have gone back to the source. I have drunk from the well and I thank him for that. But I am not sure if I am in agreement with some of what I have read. It challenges my presumptions, toys with my 50+ years of preconceived notions. I think he would tell me that was exactly his point. Be confused. Be disturbed. Get defiant. Learn.

It seems that there are a number of books that have a lot to say about this millennial-plus population of women. Some make me want to run screaming from the computer. Check out *The End of Sex: How Hookup Culture is Leaving a Generation Unhappy, Sexually Unfulfilled, and Confused About Intimacy* by Donna Freitas, 2013 and its predecessor *Hooking Up: Sex, Dating and Relationships on Campus* by Kathleen A. Bogel, 2008. You will wonder why you have worked so hard to send your kids to college.

Some make we want to call up the authors and yell, "Wait! Did you consider *this*? What about *that*?" They each make me bonkers in their own way. But I think there is much to gain from three in particular. Sandburg's *Lean In*, Patton's *Marry Smart: Advice for Finding THE ONE*, and *The Feminine Mistake* by Leslie Bennetts. Hence, this is my own personal little book group. Be careful, since it is my group, I might throw in some historical references from the 1963 classic, *The Feminist Mystique* by Betty Freidan or Germaine Greer's *The*

Female Eunuch. It's okay—you'll survive. What they had to say then is still relevant in some ways. Like D'Ambra told me, you might learn something.

I think the essential argument is between Sandberg and Patton. I feel like they are picking a fight between the brains and the uteruses of our young women. Sandberg says:

> We hold ourselves back in ways both big and small, by lacking self-confidence, by not raising our hands, and by pulling back when we should be leaning in. We internalize the negative messages we get throughout our lives—the messages that say its wrong to be outspoken, aggressive, more powerful than men. We lower our expectations of what we can achieve . . . we compromise our career goals to make room for partners and children who may not exist yet. We can dismantle the hurdles in ourselves today. We can start this very moment.[1]

I love this "go get 'em, girl" attitude. It *is* empowering. And I hear her point: we hold ourselves back. YES.

But Patton takes that empowerment and says it is being misdirected:

> I know too many brilliant, successful women who invest too many years developing *only* their career. They reach their thirties and realize that its almost impossible to find a suitable husband—*the one*—especially with their biological clocks ticking louder and faster each year. Many of them wind up single and miss their opportunity for motherhood . . . no corporate achievement,

> impressive title, or astronomical salary can compensate a woman who learns that she's waited too long and can no longer bear her own children.[2]

Before Sandberg was COO and made it her mission to advance the banner, Bennetts wrote:

> That you can't be a successful professional unless you commit to it a hundred and ten percent for your whole life—that's just wrong. The idea that the women's movement sold women a bill of goods by saying that you can have family and have real work—well, you *can*. It's true; there are millions of women who do it every day. We all know that middle class and lower class women manage to have both wage labor and families. It's only the elite women who somehow lack that capacity. The best and the brightest are somehow incapable of doing this—I mean, hello? I just think it's such a myth.[3]

I *love* this. Read it again and think of every medical technician or service manager, or teacher you have encountered who is divorced and working to support her two or three kids. How do they do it without an MBA from Wharton?

Bennetts mines the idea that women can "have it all" for an essential truth. She says for "professional women who derive an important part of their identity from their work, the whole concept of "having it all" often seems ludicrous, because it is assumed to have relevance only to females. No one ever questions a man's right to have a family as well as doing meaningful work; nobody ever talks about men "having it all" just because they've managed to sire children and hold down a paying job. (Seriously! Can you imagine someone saying to Michael Bloomberg "Mr. Mayor, How did you ever manage to build an empire when you had two daughters to raise at the same time?")

Bennets goes on to say the phrase "having it all" implies a set formula for a successful life, but every woman's interests, ambitions and personality are different, and any solution to the challenge of combining work and family is necessarily individual.[4] Of course it is. Do we all drink coffee with milk and one sugar? For that matter, do we all even drink *coffee*? I think not.

Patton echoes the sentiment that "having it all" is different for different women, but says, "the definition is always heavily skewed toward professional accomplishment, with home and family occupying whatever sliver can be shoved into the equation."[5]

Sandberg encourages women to join *her* team and "lean in," while Patton is recruiting for the old home team. (*Please stop swearing, ladies, and learn how to cook.* Puh-leeeeze!)

In our efforts to empower our daughters, we encourage them to pursue whatever interests them. Not to be afraid. Sandberg cautions:

> Fear is at the root of so many barriers that women face. Fear of not being liked. Fear of the wrong choice. Fear of drawing negative attention. Fear of overreaching. Fear of being judged. Fear of failure. And the holy trinity of fear: the fear of being a bad mother/wife/daughter.[6]

Fear of the wrong choice is exactly where Patton plunges in her traditional values dagger:

> Young women need better advice than they are being given. I encourage *every* young woman to take advantage of every new opportunity . . . but maybe not at the expense of one of our oldest and most fundamental dreams. So if marriage and children are important to you, make them every bit as important as professional success and achievement.[7]

And don't miss the opportunity to learn how to make her meatloaf (page 212 of *Marry Smart*)!

Patton also makes a strident call for women to move forward, but in a completely different direction. FEAR NOT! Find that man. Find him NOW. In college when you will never again have such wide pickin's of intellectually equal nebbish-y boy-men. You can do it. You can do it all. Have babies without the help of advanced fertility methods (by starting earlier). Have a stunning career. A fine home. Make goat cheese (page 226, I am *NOT* kidding).

Sandberg wants young women in Corporate America to lean into their career goals, to sit at the table and achieve the highest professional status, develop important mentors and, oh, by the way, don't forget about your fertility. And maybe even find a husband who will share half the housework and more of the childcare. While Sandberg wants our daughters to rule the boardroom, Patton wants them to forage for a mate "who will not be threatened by your capacity for greatness."[8]

WHAT ARE THEY TALKING ABOUT?! Our daughters have been raised in a climate of choice. They are not all brilliant corporate strategists *or* Holly Homemakers. Bennetts speaks to the need for individuality and psychiatrist and author Anna Fels addresses it in the introduction of her book *Necessary Dreams: Ambition in Woman's Changing Lives*:

> It falls nearly entirely on the individual woman to carve out a life for herself with adequate meaning and satisfactions—not an easy task for anyone, let alone an impressionable young person. For each woman life must be a creation of sorts and also an assertion of values, priorities, and identity, because no role is accepted unquestionably.[9]

I like this lady. But it leaves me wondering why this actually has to be articulated? Is it not a basic assumption for how all young people should find their place in the world, despite gender?

As I read Sandberg and Patton's tomes for the thirty-something set, I couldn't help but wonder what qualifies them as experts on the development of young women, anyway, any more than my mother, with her incessant whisper to have "something to fall back on." As a matter of record, Sandberg recounts her academic and work history and nowhere does it include developmental psychology or gender studies.

Patton's book was the (mercenary) result of a letter she wrote to the Princeton University newspaper bemoaning the fact that young women of her alma mater did not aspire to marriage and motherhood, earning her the moniker "Princeton Mom." She is a Human Resources professional. Patton even goes so far as to say in the opening pages of her book that she didn't feel the need to present statistics, she was simply giving advice based on her observations. *Really?* They may both be smart as hell, because they have sold many, many books and have made a lot of money (Sandberg's profits go to the Lean In Foundation), but I don't think their ideas are helping young women at all.

In trying to better understand both these positions, I thought it was important to return to the source and, as I said earlier, to drink from the well. And that well is Betty. Betty Friedan. Remember her? I wish Betty had been my aunt or my neighbor; I don't think I could have handled her as a mother but I sure wish I had known her when I was growing up. She was brilliant, exciting, funny. Direct. I think she would have slapped me upside my head and told me to take that same self-pitying head out of my ass and pointed me in the right direction. I think if I had known Betty then, my life would have been very different. I can't say it would have been better, but *different*. Never too late to read an old book—and find new things to learn.

In the introduction to the tenth anniversary edition of *The Feminine Mystique*, she wrote:

> The mystique we had to rebel against when it was used to confine us to the home, to keep us from developing and using our full personhood in society, distorted those real values women are now embracing, with new power and zest, both in the privacy of the home and in the larger society. And in so doing, they are changing the political and personal dimensions of marriage and families, home and the society they share with men.

Yes—YES, THEY ARE. And this is the problem I am trying to understand.

"Childbearing was never intended by biology as a compensation for neglecting all other forms of fulfillment and achievement," said Germaine Greer in 1970's *The Female Eunuch.* "It was never intended to be as time-consuming and self conscious a process as it is."[10] But it has become that. Just ask a helicopter mom on the Upper West Side of Manhattan or the 40-year-old Vice President of Marketing for some mid-size software company in AnyCity, America while she is sitting in her doctor's office at some fertility clinic waiting for test results. Having kids and raising them has been elevated to the level of extreme sport.

We still have far to go when women are bombarded with books like *Lean In* and *Marry Smart* that tell them to live *this* way or behave *that* way. It is hard enough to navigate all the choices feminism has brought, and anyone with a computer and an opinion can write a book nowadays (see example herewith ☺). But Freidan's words still ring true:

> I think this has been the unknown heart of women's problems in America for a long time, this lack of private image. Public images that . . . have very little to do with women themselves have had the power to shape too much of their lives. These images would not have such power, if women were not suffering a crisis of identity.[11]

So who *are* we and what *should* we be doing with our most fertile years? Bennetts' book predates Sandberg and Patton by about 5 years and generously references Dr. Fels, but has a simple response: "There is no one-size-fits-all answer to the question of how to achieve the right balance between career and children."[12] Thank YOU, Ms. Bennets.

One book makes you taller, one book makes you smaller; either way our daughters go down the rabbit hole trying to make their mark on careers at the cost of fertility and couplehood, or they couple and parent early and lose precious time in the race up the corporate ladder. How can we help them navigate this maze, if at all?

THREE

It's Biology, Baby: The Big Kahuna

I have so many questions and want answers. I meet with my book group—16 years together and still counting—and start badgering the ladies. We are 8 women with 7 daughters among us, from 29-37 years old. Only 1 is married. None have children. They don't need me to jab my finger at this. It is a tender spot for all of us. For the most part, our girls are not in relationships. Not only aren't they getting married, they aren't even coupling. And they certainly aren't having babies. Have we done something *wrong*? They have no answers. But how will we become grandmas, I ask them? To be honest: I whine.

"Relax," they say. Your son is married. You'll get a grandchild. *Chill.* Anyone who knows me will happily acknowledge that chilling is not my strong suit.

What is it anyway, that drives my desire, my need to hold and hug something, some*one*? To have my arms wrapped around a warm and alive being? My dog is no longer a puppy and snuggles only on her own uppity terms—a morning tummy rub, a kiss on the nose upon my return to the house. I can't get more than a cursory hug out of the kids, and my husband, the very last of the generation born in the 1940s, could hardly be called demonstrative. It isn't in his DNA. His mother stopped hugging him around puberty because, as she claimed, "It wasn't healthy for a young man to hug his mother *that* way."

What way? What she meant was that he shouldn't feel the press of her breasts.

But it is more than warm physical contact. I could get more of that, if I wanted it, as many woman who are never touched in a loving way do: through manicures, pedicures and massage. *(Why do you think there is a shop on every corner and business is booming? Think about it: one hour of socially acceptable paid intimate human contact. Where else can a woman have her hands caressed, her instep rubbed, ten minutes of back massage and walk out without having to cook a meal for the giver or pick up their underwear?)*

But this is something more. I think this is about a deeper psychology for me, a passage into psychologist Erik Erikson's Stage of Life[1] known as "Generativity," loosely defined as the time in life when an adult has a desire to pass on some of what they have learned to the next generation. And I will add to that my own believe that we have a biological determinant to pass on knowledge, culture, and yes—prepare yourself, this gets hokey: love.

The Foundation for Grandparenting website[2] says:

> Grandparenthood and great-grandparenthood may be viewed as mature stages in a lifelong developmental process. Grandparents are formed by the interaction of many biological, psychological, interpersonal and social forces . . . [they] are both born and made. This phenomenon has been recognized by many cultures. The Hindu religion accords individuals who achieve this life stage the status of "Sage," or wise one.

Ahhh, were that this was true in contemporary American life.

But back to the book group: I want to get to the bottom of this. Why are so many of our daughters still uncoupled? And where *are* the grandchildren? I am on a mission to find answers.

I am thinking hard about how to begin. I voice my frustration to my dear friend Nancy Amsel, nurse extraordinaire, who practices and teaches at the New York University Fertility Center, and helps make babies through advanced chemistry. What do you think is going on, I ask her, mother of two grown sons *(one married, zero grandchildren)*.

"I can't tell you," she said. "But we sure are busy at the Center. Why don't you talk to Dr. Keefe?"

Dr. David Keefe is an interesting fellow. A Harvard graduate with a medical degree from Georgetown University School of Medicine, he completed a residency in Psychiatry at Harvard before completing his residency in Obstetrics and Gynecology and Reproductive Medicine at Yale. A gynecologist who is also a shrink! YES! Not only is he brilliant, he is intuitive. And prolific. He has several U.S. patents and has published more than 150 papers and abstracts. But that's not what I'm talking about; when I say prolific, I mean *prolific*. The guy has SEVEN children, three of whom are daughters. He *gets* it.

Help me understand, Dr. Keefe! I tell him I am not a gender studies professor, or a sociologist, or a doctor or a scientist. I am a mother and a writer trying to understand why the successful, competent, beautiful young women I know are not finding husbands. And he tells me, "This is not a scientific story. This is a *human interest* story." And I am putty in the palm of his hand. Answers, please.

"What happened is that we were really effective at preventing conception," he says. "[This] was the most significant development in mankind. Before that, it was almost impossible for women to have fuller careers. Because we have the option of uncoupling reproduction and relationships, we have created this Pandora's Box."

I feel like I have stepped into the chamber of the Big Kahuna of reproduction, which I have. Read it again: *we have the option of uncoupling reproduction and relationships.* That's HUGE and terrifying! But this Master of Babymaking believes deeply not just in the science, but also in the humanity of his practice.

"I have a fascination for the narrative in people's lives. What they say is that people are living in the moment now. They were taught by their moms and older sisters not to squander this opportunity [for careers]. They are living out their mothers' dreams, but their mothers fail to convey the deep satisfaction women get from mothering and grandmothering.

This generation has their own brand of feminism. Some of my nurses are walking away [from their careers] now. It's their right," he says. "True feminism is the right to walk away from a career."

We talk about feminism for a few minutes and how it got a bad name. And we talk about freedom. "True *freedom*," he says, "is the ability to choose what you want . . . " And then here it comes! The hammer drops like a thousand ton weight: "Unfortunately, there is a biological clock. It's not subtle. It's not fair. *Biologically* it's not fair. And it's not the same for men."

BOOM! CRASH!

So, are you telling me that men and women can be equal

in every respect, but when it comes to reproductive parity, it just ain't fair?

"Let me tell you a story." He pushes forward across his desk leaning onto his elbows, chin cradled in his hand. His eyes are kindly; his face softens. "A patient is dating a guy. He's often in Finance or Architecture. Time goes by, and they are making money and having fun. Usually a friend asks, 'When is he going to do it? When is this guy going to move [to propose]?' Not infrequently, the guy breaks the news that he is having an affair and he is going to marry his [younger] secretary. This happens *often*. The harsh reality of this is that [women] have lost years. And then they are here." By *here*, Dr. Keefe means they are physically in his clinic, electing to freeze their eggs. And it doesn't always work. There's a specific formula involving patient age for *potential* success, as the NYU Fertility Center[3] brochure points out:

> Fertility preservation through oocyte (egg) freezing allows women to store eggs at a younger age for use when they are older and is now a viable option . . . to date, there are over 2,000 births worldwide (greater than 1,000 reported in the last five years) as a result of egg freezing.
>
> The process involves stimulating eggs in the woman's ovaries and then harvesting and storing those eggs for use at a later date. Oocyte quality is best when a woman is in her reproductive prime (age 16 to 28). Many eggs are usually still of good quality in the mid-reproductive years (age 29 to 38) and may remain usable (but with

> diminished chance for producing pregnancy) in the late-reproductive period (age 39 to 44). If necessary or desired, it is best to have eggs that are frozen when they are of the best quality possible. For instance, eggs frozen at the age of 35 are more usable than fresh oocytes produced at 43 years of age.

In an article titled "Ova Easy: Egg Freeze Calculator" that appeared in the NY Post on June 2, 2013, Susan Edelman wrote:

> Dr. Kutluk Oktay of New York Medical College, a division of the Touro College and University System has led a team that crunched data from 2,265 egg-freezing cycles in 1,805 women in the US and Europe.
>
> The data suggest that women planning to store their eggs should get cracking. According to the calculator, a 21-year-old who freezes a dozen eggs, the average number, has a 43 percent shot at giving birth when she's ready to get pregnant. A 45-year-old has only a 12 percent chance.
>
> The key is a woman's age when she freezes her eggs—not when she wants to get pregnant.

Dr. Keefe says, "It becomes a tsunami of concerns and worries that have been suppressed and minimized . . . the idea of what makes a successful career woman. They can go through seven or eight freeze cycles. As a therapist, we see this. It's a major conundrum. The women do everything right. They are following the rules, but the rules are not made for them. Guys can goof off their whole lives, break up with the girlfriend when they are 50 and still marry and have kids with someone 30." He delivers this truth with a deep sadness in his voice. "It is really important for women to be aware of the clock."

Dr. Keefe sites his wife, Candace Hasey Keefe, as an example of someone who made some of the hard choices. "She was a news anchor. She had a big career and she walked away from it. It's all myths. She never for a moment wavered from her commitment to wanting kids. She never deluded herself that it was anything more than a job. Your kids are forever."

Candy agrees. "I always wanted a large family. It was a goal of mine since I was a child." Trained as a teacher at Boston College with a master's degree in education from Harvard *(a degree one can fall back on!)* she changed her mind about teaching along the way and switched to communications after doing some fieldwork for a television production class. With a new focus, she went to Stanford for a master's degree in journalism. Working long, hard hours, she worked her way up to Producer in a very short time and got her shot at an on-air position, earning two Emmys along the way. Oh yes, she also got married and had five children. She worked full-time while her husband completed his residency and several fellowships.

"I breastfed every kid for a year," she says, and went back to work quickly after each birth. "The kids did very well with good nannies." As the kids got older and she added two more to her family, she felt they needed her at home. "The bigger the kids, the bigger the issues." Candy's own mother was a stay-at-home mom who only went back to work when she and her three sisters were older. "I saw this was something you could do. Nothing was said about getting married and having kids, but more about doing what makes you happy.

"Jobs will come and go," Candy independently echoes her husband's words, "but your family is here to stay. That's the message I have given my children."

Sheryl Sandburg is screaming in my ear at this point. "*Lean in! Lean in!* See: you *can* do it all. You just need good help." Yeah—good nannies or a good wife. We all need a wife at home so we can pursue our professional desires and still get the downstairs toilet fixed and the kids to the orthodontist. I always thought I would like a wife who would do the laundry and make salad every night for dinner. Washing lettuce is *such* a drag and it never helped anyone's intellectual or emotional development.

"I love my job. But if I had to choose, I wouldn't hesitate for a second," Dr. Keefe concedes. But he is not a woman, and although he has had a wonderful, independently accomplished wife caring for his brood, he worries about his daughters and our daughters. "If women can just learn they have only one life. We spend a lot of time helping women break free of all the rules, to help them be the skipper of their own ship. It's hard."

Admittedly, The NYU Fertility Clinic sees a very specific and particular population. They are one of the best in the city, the country . . . the *world*. Their clientele are well-educated and for the most part, financially able to afford the help. I ask if this is, specifically, a Metropolitan Female Executive (a "*Lean In*" girls') problem, and he tells me it is not just a New York issue.

"It's in all major metropolitan areas. China is now doing more IVF than anywhere else. They are bumping up against negative population growth with fewer and fewer young people. There are IVF centers popping up all over." A sought-after speaker across the globe, "It's a worldwide issue," he explains.

"It does tend to be more educated women, and tends toward cities." He also points out there is a "binary distribution: less-educated populations tend to marry earlier . . . there is a growing schism between highly educated and less fertile women and the less educated and more fertile. They are co-dependent. Fertility has become a commodity. Literally. You can go online and buy eggs, frozen and stored . . . you can go to sperm bank websites and choose celebrity look-alikes." In Florida, they are finding a large population of women who are interested in being surrogates for women unable to carry their own biological child. Some are 25 years old and have already had three children. Their wombs are for rent.

But the educated woman has the potential to become "the empowered woman. We are as capable as men," says Candy, "but we are *not* men. There is a balance to be maintained." When she worked in Texas she noticed a big difference between the women of her hometown, Boston, and the southern ladies. "Where I came from, women didn't wear makeup, but Dallas was completely different. All these beautiful people. They were *into* the difference between the sexes."

I had many questions for Dr. Keefe. Did he think there was someone or something to blame? Did feminism sell women an empty promise of great careers with disregard for marriage, natural conception and childrearing? Are men (biologically) driven to abandon same-aged mates for more fertile options? He cites this oft-quoted observation from philosopher and visionary Buckminster Fuller: "There is a simple truth: that every system does what it is designed to do. If a different outcome is desired, then the system must be changed." He said that the sociological implications are vast but the great thing is "women have options."

I didn't feel I had options when I was 21. The only girl between two brothers, one elevated to genius status because of his high IQ and eccentric personality, the other plagued by the emotional rejection of our father *(long story . . . different book)*. I knew my path. It was mapped out for me from a very early age.

"Why waste money on college for you," my father declared. "You'll only end up pregnant and a housewife."

"What do you mean you want to be a writer," my mother said. "That's not a career for a woman. Be a teacher. Like me. You can always earn a living, if you have to." Something to fall back on. The respectable path for smart Jewish girls who were on track for marriage and family. Even though my mother figured out how to leave and move forward (and stop at the campus bar for a drink after class with her cute young friends) while I was making dinner, she didn't instill a forward-thinking mentality in me. There was such an assumption I would be abandoned. What little faith.

So, options? Yes. But for a narrow span of a woman's lifetime. With the biological clock tick-tocking away through month after month of unproductive menstrual cycles, and the lifespan increasing year after year, a young woman today must make reproductive choices within a specific 15-20 year period or she may be looking at a long and possibly lonely life without offspring. *(I know, I know . . . I hear you, feminists: assuming she even wants a baby.)*

Add to that burden, Sandburg says these are the very same years a woman must "lean in" if she wants that high profile career. How far have we *really* come?

I call my daughter and share with her the findings from my interview with Dr. Keefe. I am pie-eyed by the amazing fact that the day a woman is born, she loses 80% of her eggs. Every day we lose more eggs, Dr. Keefe tells me. I am dumbfounded by the enormity of this information. I tell her that peak fertility is between 20 and 25 years and stays constant until age 30, when there is a subtle decline.

"What are you telling me?" she asks. "You want me to go out and try and get pregnant before the eggs are gone?" No, no, no . . . I say. Yes, I think. I am afraid she will miss the joy of having a baby and raising a family. (She had a very brief marriage to an awful man and got out before there were children. No dummy, my kid. So why have *I* so little faith?)

I continue to impart my newly acquired information. From age 35-38, a woman's fertility begins to decline and after 38, "it drives off a cliff," says Keefe. But there is a heritable factor, he explains. There are active studies being conducted in the Ultra Orthodox Jewish community, where women have seventeen children and are still willing to go another round. "There is a real genetic factor. They are working on isolating the gene," Dr. Keefe informs me.

"If a mother has babies at a later age, that bodes well for her daughter's fertility," I repeat to my daughter. "I had your brother at 37."

"I remember," she rolls her eyes. "I was there." Changing diapers. Feeding bottles. She doesn't have to say it out loud. I hear it ricochet within the vacant potholes in my brain. Three months after my youngest was born, I tripped while carrying him down a short flight of stairs and had a severe ankle break. Six months and seven pieces of hardware later, my daughter learned that motherhood is hard. She started early, too.

The ankle break precipitated my own mother's nervous

breakdown. Already emotionally volatile, my indisposition put her over the edge. If I was the one who could be counted on, and I was broken, who was there to keep her stable? She took a leave of absence from her job and moved into the basement of our 1,500 square foot cottage, with three kids under seven, the nanny (who didn't like to clean) and my husband and myself. To say it was crowded would be a polite euphemism.

Our lives consisted of me yelling schedules from the couch while fielding phone calls to and from my mother's therapist and administering her meds. In my heart of hearts, if I could have gotten up from that couch and walked into a classroom of snarky middle schoolers right then and there, I would have considered teaching something wonderful to fall back on. But there was no classroom awaiting me, only the complications of family life as an incapacitated wife and mother. So I ask myself again, what message did I impart to my daughter?

Did I tell her how amazing it is to carry a child and give birth? To nourish that baby from your own body? Did I describe the insurmountable joy of watching an infant develop from a wheezing, mucus machine who sneezes, gasps and poops all day into a bright-eyed toddler who would one day become a Paleo-eating, Cross-fit training CFO at the age of 24? No, I didn't. I didn't have the wisdom or the foresight. I told her only that she should grow up and have a great job so she might make her own choices about career and motherhood. I did a good job, a really good job of convincing her that although it might be nice to have a family, it certainly wasn't the end goal.

There is much more to learn. Dr. Keefe has recommended that I speak to several other professionals in the field of reproduction and women's bodies. Armed with their email addresses, my search for understanding continues.

THE FRENCH CONNECTION

Margaux and Christiane. Two lovely French women have agreed to speak with me. A mother and daughter, who compared to the American women I have spoken with, seem to have an idyllic philosophy about getting married and having babies.

Christiane says her mother encouraged her to find happiness when she was growing up, to always "stay true" to herself. "She really showed me what was important for her to be happy [and] getting married and having kids is really important, but so was doing something you love. And she kept telling me studying was important."

Margaux was a stay-at-home mom with five children who did a lot of charitable work. After 23 years, she went back to work outside the home out of necessity, but enjoyed it so much she stayed by choice. Her own mother encouraged her to have a simple happy life. She grew up in an economically secure home with two happy parents. Her father also encouraged the idea of a happy life.

"Happiness is important, work is important, education is important, but family is more important," she says. With all that happiness in the family, it is interesting that her early career aspiration was "to become a nun and then a stay-at-home mom." Instead of a vocation in the most traditional sense, she got married, worked for two years and then had her five children.

Christiane aspired to be a paleontologist and then an archeologist, but "I always thought that I wanted to get married and have kids. As a girl, it was mandatory for me to get married at some point." She got the message loud and clear: "You could not be happy, if you weren't married and didn't have kids." Now a career woman in New York City, she says, "I haven't met the right person but I am not focusing on finding a partner. The most important thing for me right now is finding things that make me happy, [and] to travel. But finding a partner would be an added bonus."

Unlike her mother, Christiane does not think she will stop working to raise her children. "Maybe a few years when they are very little, unless my partner wants to be a stay-at-home dad."

Margaux recognizes the movement from generation to generation. "Contrary to my mother, I started to work again. Contrary to my daughter, I stopped work to raise my kids. I don't think my daughter will do that."

Christiane understands her biological clock and would be open to adoption if she found her partner after her chance of conception had passed, but at 27 she says, "I would like to meet the right person, yes, but this is not taking priority over my life."

After talking to Dr. Keefe, I wonder if she knows the risk she is taking.

FOUR

It's Biology, Baby: The Pragmatic Pathologist

It is a sultry summer day and I have just finished one interview and am scooting across midtown Manhattan to meet distinguished researcher and professor, Dr. Larry Landsman[1]. His curriculum vitae could be a chapter onto itself, but like Dr. Keefe, his friend and colleague who made the introduction for me, he is much more than his credentials. Landsman holds both an M.D. and a Ph.D. in cellular biochemistry from an Ivy League university. He is currently a research scientist in the Department of Obstetrics and Gynecology at another Ivy League school and serves as director of their Reproductive Research Unit with a special interest in infertility and pregnancy complications. His first question to me takes me off guard.

"So what's *your* story?" he asks me, his intense eyes peering at me from behind round wire-rimmed glasses. He wears a fully executed tie at the collar of his pristine white shirt, the cuffs of his sleeves folded back twice, with a crisp edge, to allow for a cooling breeze. He conveys an aura of immaculate precision and surgical sterility, supported by an under layer of fierce intelligence and suppressed humor. Yes—humor. I was sure the jokes would pop out at any given moment. And they did. In the hour and a half we spend together, he makes me laugh and he makes me cry.

He is actually interested in how I came to be there, interviewing him. I give him the short version: New Jersey born and bred. Syracuse University. Met my husband as counselors at summer camp in the Catskills. Married at 22, first baby at 26. 4 children. 1 stillborn. I don't usually volunteer that information, but since he is a researcher who investigates difficult pregnancies, I deem it safe. I count on his professional manner to not go all "Oh, no—poor you!" on me. And he doesn't. He asks specific questions and in no time at all we are deeply into issues of fertility and why so many women in their thirties are not marrying or having babies.

First and foremost, Landsman wants to identify as the father of three daughters, each single and of age for my study, and the son of a "potent female." His mother, Sarah who passed away in 2011, was a highly respected literary scholar and "a radical feminist," says Landsman. His aunt worked on the Manhattan Project.

"I grew up with amazing women and this model of the potent female . . . my mother is the reason I have this attitude about women. [She said,] 'Do not just have sex with a girl in the back of a car. Love her.'"

Define it for me, this "potent female," I request. It sounds a little threatening. Like it's contagious, or maybe explosive. *Dangerous.* He explains that a "potent female" in his world is a strong, determined woman who is not looking to outside sources for acceptance or permission. She is independent and goes out into the world to do what she wants to do. She doesn't need a man to actualize herself. This is powerful stuff and most of the women I have interviewed and many of Landsman's patients fit this description (congratulations, Betty Freidan: ya done good.).

Landsman is married to potent female, Jane. They met in

college when he was doing post-graduate work and she was working for an administrative branch of the same university. "She was interesting," he says. "We had lunch together for six months" until both of them left other relationships to be together. They are both "take charge" people who find the time to take care of each other. Jane has a high-powered, demanding career and their three daughters have grown up seeing "two fully independent people with actualized lives and highly accomplished behaviors and actions." He riffs on their childhood, being at home to see them through the typical adolescent issues. "I'm the one who bought tampons with them. I am their front line in terms of personal and emotional things." He has more to say about raising daughters, but you will have to wait for the chapter about Dads. I want to get to the meat and potatoes of our conversation: the mating game.

Landsman says that men are basically afraid of potent females. "This is what I tell my women students: *it's biology*. The only thing that makes a relationship work is that the man wants the female. The job of the female is to choose which male they let in. This is truly our biology. Men are pretty indiscriminate—but they have to *want* that female."

He continues to state that the biggest mistake an interested female can make is going after a male partner. "Listen, a couple hooks up. Just who is getting what? If the female is willing to give the guy a blowjob, that's cool. But I ask my women [students]: was there pleasure in it for you? No. So what are you getting out of it? They think that if they have given the guy sexual pleasure he will respond to them. If you have milk every day, why do you have to buy the cow?" It's a phrase as old as our grandmothers and not worthy of a man raised by a potent female; it's a degrading image, to say the least.

So what are you telling me, I ask? A woman can't find a mate unless he chooses her first?

"The only way this works is that they have to be around those males." Oh lordy, I think. Is Princeton Mom *right*? Say it isn't so, Dr. Landsman.

"This is biology," he explains. "A neuro-endocrine process that's happening. Dopamine, pair-bonding. The male is fighting for the female. The female chooses from amongst the suitors. When they have sex and she has an orgasm, it releases oxytocin and she bonds to him. It's a selection process. The orgasm is a test to make women feel safe enough . . . in a trusted environment the orgasm starts the advance bonding that enables her to attach to him. It's all driven hormonally."

"But . . . but . . . " What about the "hooking up" orgasm? The masturbation orgasm? Where's the bonding there?

"There is no 'but,'" he says. "Biology trumps. And in places where [a woman] is just being viewed, the physical trumps. It is important to see how someone behaves. Are their actions attractive? There has to be a trigger. There has to be a biological basis: does their behavior harmonize with the man, can they see themselves with this woman? They need to get to the essence of the issue immediately." **STOP IT!** You are *killing* me. It can't be all about dressing up and twitching your hips, I say.

"It is the biology of millions of years of evolution," says Landsman. "We are animals and this is how animals work."

I am overcome by the enormity of what he is saying. I feel tears welling up. Can it be so simple? So disheartening? What about all the smart, beautiful women I know who spend hours on computer dating sites, hours sitting across from men they meet up with at Starbucks, at wine bars, at the Highline?

Do they have no choice? Are they just waiting to be *chosen*? It smacks of the 1960s. All the wallflowers at the middle school dances, dressed in their best party clothes, lined up in chairs. Waiting. Waiting for the nice guys like Jack Muller or Mike Braun to give them a pity dance while the hot girls flash their panties as they execute elaborate moves on the dance floor. How far have we come if we are still waiting to be chosen?

"These women have bought into the idea that they could *chose*," Landsman says. "What females need to do in order to find a partner is this: they need to be out there. Do what you love to do. You will be with others who love to do what you love to do. You have to circulate in the right target environment."

I can't believe this is what he is telling me: that our daughters can only put themselves out there and wait to be chosen.

"It's just the way it is. She cannot, nor can any woman, choose a man . . . the relationship lasts only as long as the man wants to stay in the relationship . . . we can't dismiss biology."

I argue some more about self-determination and self-actualization. I argue passionately and pleadingly—for my daughter, for all the daughters of all the women I have interviewed. A few tears roll down my cheek as I try to process it against all the feminist literature I have been reading. I simultaneously understand and reject the implications of what he is saying.

"You can try and put social or psychological overlays on a biological system, but it doesn't work. Biology trumps," he says with finality. The sky is darkening outside the cafe, and the air thickens with electricity. Landsman looks at a weather app on his phone.

"The storm is moving quickly. We've got about 20 minutes," he says. We signal for the check. I pack up my computer.

We head outside to look for a cab.

"Thank you so much," I gush, grateful for the time this busy scientist has given me, even if I am not happy with the information he has imparted. I extend my hand to shake.

Larry opens his arms. "C'mon, let's have a hug!" he says. I don't feel quite so bad.

EXITING IOWA

One of 12 siblings aged 36 to 52, Lila is a personable, petite, curvaceous man-magnet. At 45, she still has all the goods. I know this because she is a friend of mine and we have been many places together. Without fail, men's heads swivel for a long look. (Yes: biology. I have been told that they can't help it.) Half German and half Irish, Lila's cool blonde looks, upturned nose and glistening smile have gotten us the best table and free drinks. It's fun to hang with her; it's always a good time. But many goodtime gals hold deep sadness within, and Lila is no exception.

Growing up as the fourth daughter, she was often the caretaker for the younger siblings. The home was so busy there wasn't time (or inclination) to discuss the joys or difficulties of marriage and motherhood.

"I don't remember my mother ever saying anything about this . . . we rarely spoke about anything," Lila tells me. "We were not close at all." But she learned child-rearing and homemaking skills nevertheless. "I was taught how to care for a newborn all the way up to toddler and beyond . . . but this didn't come only from my mother. My older sisters taught me a lot as well . . . and I also learned by observation."

The family started out as middle class, but deteriorated

financially after her parents divorced. Her mother was not a happy woman. Such a large family "left little time for her to do anything else but tend to everyone else's needs . . . my father was an alcoholic for as long as I can remember, as well as quite the philanderer . . . so that made things very difficult for everyone." The divorce sent them from comfortable middle class to welfare-dependent, forcing her mother to take a job outside the home to make ends meet.

Although her father was present when she was growing up, after the divorce he "disappeared for several years. When he reappeared, he had gone through rehab and was sober. Then he was around once a month or so. He lived about 50 miles away from us at that time. As a group, we kids were not all that excited to see him or spend time with him at that point anyway." She doesn't know what led her father "to the bottle. He never talked about that."

Despite the discord between her parents, Lila says they managed to instill a very strong work ethic in their children and it has served her well. "We all worked for everything we had. I started working when I was 14 and have paid for everything I have on my own ever since."

Lila had dreams of her own, though. "I thought I would get married to an amazing man, have two or three beautiful kids and be happy somewhere far, far away from my parents." But that is not what happened. "NOT EVEN CLOSE! I am as far away from what I thought would happen as anyone could get. I had a chance to get married . . . I've been asked six times. I was engaged once . . . and I broke off the engagement two weeks before the wedding. He was the amazing man I thought I would spend the rest of my life with . . . but when it came right down to it, I couldn't do it. I was too young—19 going on 20—and I wanted to see the world . . . and do things that I had never done. Hell, I didn't even know what those things were that I wanted to do, I just knew that if I got married when I was supposed to . . . I would never be able to do what I wanted to do. I think deep down, I was terrified of ending up like my mom had. Stuck. In the middle of nowhere with nothing to do and no options."

When we talk about feminism, equality, and options, Lila says "Oh man . . . that one is complicated. Feminism to me, in the workplace, is that each person . . . male and female, should be given an opportunity based solely on their ability and qualifications. Their sex should be a non-issue. However, in my personal life, I want a man who is a 'gentleman,' with old-fashioned manners. A man who holds the door, and gets my chair at the dinner table, and stands when I stand to leave or return, and helps me put my coat on and who pays for dinner. To me, these things are not pandering to the female sex . . . but instead it tells me that this man wants to make me feel safe and that he is respectful of women."

Lila is an independent woman, with a BFA and a strong job history, but still, she would like a partner with whom to share her life. Although at one time she didn't want children, she has changed her mind.

"Early on in my twenties, I didn't want to have children for many reasons. I was very close to my baby brother who died. My parents were going through the toughest part of the divorce and neither one of them was ever around. I was the oldest at home and taking care of everyone, literally! I got everyone up for school and made breakfast, lunch and dinner when they all came home. I did laundry and got them ready for bed, and then did my homework. Jimmy was three going on four. My senior year of high school, he went everywhere with me except to my classes. I normally would have been a cheerleader and on the track team and the softball team. But that year, I did none of those things. I took care of my siblings. Jimmy and I became more like a mother/son than a sister/brother. When he died a few years later, part of me died with him. I was devastated for a very long time. Taking care of my brothers and younger sister for so long, I felt like I had gone through being a parent already . . . all except the actual childbirth. I wasn't in a hurry to do that again."

Age changed her outlook. "I wanted to be a mom. I have been pregnant twice. I miscarried both times in the eighth week. My first pregnancy, I was 37 years old. I was with someone when I got pregnant and then we broke up before I found out. The second time, I was 43 and had been with someone for 5 years. The miscarriage was the catalyst for breaking up."

At this point in her life, she has already pursued alternative paths to pregnancy. "I have been through all the tests for in vitro. I am not a candidate. My body doesn't produce enough eggs. I *am* open to adoption . . . I think having a child when there are two loving people or more around is ideal, but not necessary. I think—hell—I *know* from experience, children know and feel when they are loved. It isn't about the amount of people, it's about the amount of love."

Lila would still like to meet someone with whom to share her life. "I am hopeful. I would LOVE to have someone to share my life with, the ups, downs and in-betweens, someone to make my heart race when I think about seeing them, who makes the highs higher and the lows not so bad because they are by my side. I know it's a romantic view on relationships, but I've had this with someone before. Maybe he was my 'one.' I don't know. All I know is that it's possible. There are always going to be problems with relationships. It's expected. It's part of a relationship evolving. I guess, what I am saying it that right now, at this point in my life, I would choose to be with someone—granted not just anyone—but someone that made me happy most of the time (and I made him happy most of the time), rather than being alone. Even that is a scary statement to make! I don't want to say I'll 'settle' for someone; there has to be enough right things between us to make dealing with their bullshit worth it. Does that make sense? Man, I sound like a hopefully pessimistic romantic!"

I press her on why she has not found someone permanent, when she attracts men like pie attracts flies. "I honestly have no idea. I am very busy with my own life. Don't get me wrong, dating is a priority, but I want to be able to take care of myself and not depend on a man."

Lila has a working list of factors she believes contribute to her single status that she enumerates for me:

1. I am focusing on making my career successful.
2. The majority of men my age are married already and I am not looking for someone in their twenties or thirties.
3. I have been told I am intimidating and not very approachable, which frankly doesn't bother me. It keeps many men that I wouldn't be interested in anyway at bay.

"Timing. Opportunity. Life!" she says. "I've wondered why I haven't met someone many times, but I've forced myself to not ask that question anymore because it only serves to make me crazy. If it's me, well, I am who I am and I like who I am and don't want to act like someone else to get a man or keep a man. [But] I believe life is meant to be shared with someone else and everything has more significance when it can be experienced with someone you love. If I have added joy and love to someone's life, maybe, to me, it means I had a purpose while on this earth. That's important to me."

Lila's choices have been very different from those of her mother. "She chose a very traditional route and my life is completely the opposite. I pursued my hopes and dreams and my path has not been an easy one. My mother's was difficult as well, but in a different way. I think maybe what I have learned is that any path we choose will have its challenges. It's how we react to those challenges, to try to make choices that lead us toward the most happiness is about the best we can do."

FIVE

It's Biology, Mama: Don't Waste Time!

With over 45 years on the job, Dr. Lila Nachtigall is still a force of nature, working full-time in the gynecology/obstetrics practice in New York City that she shares with her daughter, Margaret. (Another daughter is a neuro-endocrinologist, and the third is an attorney.) A worldwide expert on the role estrogen plays in a woman's body, she has written over 500 journal articles and several books, including *Estrogen*, which has become a sourcebook for others in the field. So who better to ask about the changes in women's lives than a woman who was already in medical school before Betty Freidan took the train out of Westchester.

"The first thing my mother said when I told her I wanted to go to medical school was 'No one will marry you!' She wasn't happy about it." But with the encouragement of her husband who paid her first year of tuition, she went anyway. Now married 56 years, she says her husband has encouraged her to do everything. She has been a lucky woman in that department. "I had a wonderful mother, a doting father . . . it gave me a lot of confidence to do what I wanted to do." And, along with her exceptional genetic package—she is very, very smart—she has passed this legacy on to her daughters.

"My daughters saw me. They have three children each and they work full-time, very full-time. They are all extremely accomplished . . . I always talked about my work at home. My husband, who is also a doctor, said to them 'You'll be a doctor when you grow up.' Two of them listened. I feel very successful [in my career] but also that my three daughters are happily married. It's a huge accomplishment."

Although Nachtigall bucked the system when she was starting out in an age when the majority of women set marriage and family as their primary (and often only) goal, I press her to explain to me when and how she saw things change for women.

"I saw it happening right around the time my daughters were marrying, about 22 years ago . . . it really started in the group who are now about 55. Women could do it—they got it! They didn't have to be a teacher. That wasn't the only choice." *(Oh dear, I was just a little too early!)*

I ask her if she believes that the availability of safe contraception was the turning point and she says it was a small point. "I peg it to being financially independent . . . women wanted to do it for themselves . . . I think that was the big issue. 'I want to be something first and then I will get married.' Delaying pregnancy was just a part of the picture."

She tells me about one of her fertility patients. The woman is 42 and has been married for 10 years. "I asked her why she didn't try for pregnancy before and she said she just got around to it. 'I was going to be a judge,' she told me. 'I was on track, I wanted to accomplish that first.' She forgot that [pregnancy] occurs within biology. Evolution takes a million years to change."

So what is a young woman to do now, if she wants marriage and family as well as a career? I am surprised by her answer. She says they should be looking at their classmates in college, graduate school, medical school. *(Helllooo, Princeton Mom!)*

"You see in *The New York Times* "Vows" section every week: they met in college but they are way past graduation . . . people are getting married older. It's amazing to me, it used to be 18."

We talk about Princeton Mom and Nachtigall says, "I agree with her, the women should at least be *thinking* about it. I see the benefit to it. Both my daughters met their husbands in medical school . . . the other met her husband working as an assistant district attorney . . . at [the college level] men are more immature, but if you are a freshman and he's a senior . . . even with all this social media, if you didn't meet them in college, and if you didn't go to graduate school, there is not a place to meet them."

So I push my agenda, asking her if these women have missed their chance. "Probably not, but they have to try harder. I always recommend going online. The biggest problem is the available pool . . . definitely it's easier for men. They keep going down the age scale. [For women] every year older, you get leftovers. The longer a woman is out of school, her pool is decreased. His pool is increased from puberty on . . . our culture hasn't changed very much; an older guy can go out with a younger woman, but if it goes the opposite way, people look at it funny."

I want to know if she agrees with Dr. Landsman that it is a man's choice. "No," she says definitively. "It's certainly not 100% or even 90%. He may think that as a man, but we both know a woman can go after a man . . . a man often doesn't get the hint until the woman is flirting with him, sending off her signals. I don't buy into it as an overwhelming thing. Biologically, if the man is not interested in the woman, it's not going to work. But it can go both ways. My mother had an old fashioned saying, 'She set her cap for him.'"

I ask her to tell me if there is hope for our daughters to find a mate and start a family and she assures me there is. "I think those who really want a husband, they usually find one. I have lots of women in their forties. They go online. They find them. Some go on to have babies by themselves. Some of them have wasted time with the wrong person. The over thirty-fives—that group almost always wasted time."

Her advice? "Increase your pool. Don't waste time. Find the right person."

I decide to do a brief study to see if what Nachtigall says is true about the "Vows" section in the *Times*. Already an avid reader of this portion of the paper—I am always looking for daughters and sons of people I know who have found their mate *(whew)*—I collect 3 successive weeks in September of 2014. I decide to throw out the marriages between people on the upside of 45 (a very small sampling) and focus on straight couples, as the gay marriages are a demographic outside my study.

I add together the marriages for all 3 weeks. 94 announcements meet my criteria. Of those, 31 of those couples met at college: Harvard leads the pack with 6 matches, Yale and Washington University tie with 3 marriages each. 20 colleges are represented overall, many are Ivy League. And Nachtigall is right on target: these are marriages between people who met at college but married later. There are very few spring chickens, as my grandmother used to say. Only 3 of the brides are 25. The rest are older, with 35 in their thirties and 31 of them either 28 or 29.[1]

Again, I remind myself that this is a very select population; it is a narrow study of couples living in the metropolitan New

York City area who feel strongly about having their marriage announced in such a fashion. It is very competitive to get listed. There are specific requirements for the pictures that are submitted, like the couples' eyes have to be on the same level. And the *Times* staff does a fact check on relatives listed in the announcement. I know this to be true because they called to check on the spelling of my name and confirm my employment when my son and daughter-in-law posted their nuptials. It was weird but wildly exciting to hear from long-lost friends and relatives who saw the announcement. I can't believe how many people read this drivel. *(Me!)*

I am also surprised by how Natchtigall's theory is reflected in my own life. I married the oldest of three brothers. When I look at my sisters and brothers-in-law, we are six individuals with only two colleges among us. We went either to Syracuse University or Boston University. An even split. Was it simply serendipity that we found the mate we did? Or were we destined by geography and cultural orientation?

But what does that offer me about the chances for our daughters to find a mate? Not a lot, really, except that it wouldn't be a bad idea to suggest they attend their college reunions. *Okay*, Susan Patton, you might be on to something.

If all this focus on the search for a partner is just too much, this might be a good time to introduce Dr. Stephanie Marshall Thompson. I have included her in this book for two reasons: first as a reproductive specialist, and also as a woman raised by parents with strong achievement goals for their daughter. You will meet her again in the chapter about dads, but she also presents an interesting perspective in the area of fertility options.

Thompson is a practicing reproductive endocrinologist and infertility specialist working in Northern New Jersey. She is strikingly beautiful. Tall, slim, with long elegant fingers. I know it is not professionally or socially correct from a feminist point of view to tie her physical beauty to her professional accomplishments but there is a natural visceral reaction to her appearance: she is lovely to look at. And kind, with a gentle, cultured voice and a warm smile. I imagine that an examination by Dr. Thompson would not be as reprehensible as a typical visit to the gynecologist.

When Thompson was in medical school and deciding on a specialty, she knew early on that she would choose infertility. It didn't hurt that she had a strong role model: her father is an obstetrician. Her patient base spans three communities and many demographics, serving women from 25-45, across the spectrum from retired Manhattan professional women to teachers and cops. She treats women with a variety of issues ranging from primary infertility, underlying endocrine disorders, tubal disease, uterine abnormalities and male factor infertility (which accounts for 30-40% of infertility) as well as infertility related to over-exercising and eating disorders. She also deals with those wanting sex selection, which I guess is the gynecological equivalent of rhinoplasty: procedures for those who are just not happy with what nature has provided.

"I got pregnant my first year of fellowship because I saw patients my own age with unexplained fertility issues and I took their struggle personally. It was a common trend among my colleagues, both male and female. They were in their thirties and many of them had to have fertility treatments for various reasons." She now has two children, two years apart.

Thompson and her partners actually offer a bit of a solution to the career/family question that harkens back to the Big Kahuna of infertility, Dr. Keefe, who was one of Thompson's teachers. But Thompson's practice goes a step further. Not only do they offer egg freezing on the Jersey side of the Hudson River, but they also advocate it for women who are not yet *ready* to produce offspring. They actually encourage it among college women.

"Egg freezing is freedom," says Thompson. "It takes away some of the anxiety about finding the right guy. It's part of the empowerment. You want to be with someone because you *want* to, not just because you need to. Egg freezing [while] developing a career you love takes away the stress." Now this is the first thing that sounds like a positive development for women since they introduced equal pay for equal work. Go on! Go on! I urge her.

"You don't just want to enter into a relationship that might be detrimental to you just because your friends are getting married and having babies. The only down side is it's a medical procedure that requires elective surgery, but its relatively safe."

She quotes one of the other doctors in her practice, "Egg freezing is an insurance policy, not an excuse not to develop your personal life."

There it is: if we can get our daughters through college, where they may or may not have chosen a husband from the multitude of brilliant classmates, and encourage them to freeze their eggs while their fertility is at its peak, they can then go on to graduate school without fear of never having the children they are putting off while they lean into their careers. I jest, yes. But I am not sure Dr. Thompson is very far off base.

SHORT AND NEAT

Some of the women I consult for this book do not live locally and cannot be interviewed in person, but are kind enough to complete a nosy, intrusive questionnaire for me. It is not always easy for them, as there are definitely big issues of trust. If I am a friend of their mother, or they are friends with my daughter, they have to believe that all the information they share is confidential. I know stuff about their families. For all the women, they need to decide what is safe to reveal and what is none of my business, even anonymously. Many are generous with their time and emotions and write prolifically on the topic, sharing intimate details. But I am particularly struck by two short and simple questionnaire responses. One woman, Lisa, is just living her life, not stressing about marriage and babies. The other, Kristin: not so much. But both answer in a few sentences that nevertheless come to the same place.

When I read through the responses from Kristin and Lisa I am surprised by their matter-of-fact answers: *it is what it is.* Both women come from homes with parents they consider happily married, although Kristin says her parents "fight and have communication issues, but I believe they really love and respect each other," and Lisa says her dad is "happy and grumpy, not that they are mutually exclusive."

Lisa grew up with the expectation that "you work first and play later." Her mother works in the garment industry by choice and they have a comfortable home life and have encouraged her, like so many others, to "do what makes you happy."

She confesses to "never thinking about" what would happen when she became an adult. "I was too busy in the moment." Now that she is 33, she would "love to be in a relationship, but you can't force it," and will "worry about becoming a mother" if she can find the right partner. "Until then, I want to live a happy and fulfilled life." She does not seem too concerned at all about ticking clocks or dwindling pools of men. What is of note is her reaction to the idea of fertility assistance, should she be late to the party. My question about being open to alternative paths to parenthood is met with a simple "meh." Unlike so many of my young women, she simply isn't stressing.

Kristin, on the other hand, *is*. She assumed she would have a job by now and be living with a boyfriend. At 27, she is a bit young for this study. Her expectations are evolving. She says, "I am a single medical student and still haven't started making any money of my own." But now even the idea of having children is in flux. "I'm undecided. I always imagined myself having children and the idea still gets me very excited and passionate – but it's also extremely stressful . . . I can see myself being unable to keep boundaries and separate my children's lives from my own." That's a pretty interesting and astute comment for a young woman.

When asked how she sees her life as different from her mother's, she says, "I hope I will be able to separate my life as an adult from my life as a partner, from my life as a doctor, from my life as a parent, as well as someone's daughter." That's a pretty tall challenge, and rooted in the preeminence of individuality. Her desire for that kind of compartmentalization in her life is intriguing; it is deeply shaped by the multitude of choices available for women today. It gives a powerful nod to the pioneers of the Women's Movement who led the way to opening up those options. I am sorry that Kristin's mother, who has a major career of her own, declined to be included in the study. I think we're missing out on an interesting perspective.

In the end, though, Lisa and Kristin are not so different from many of us. Men and women alike. "I hope I have some kind of meaningful relationship," Kristin says, "and someone to look forward to seeing when I get home everyday."

This seems to be an inherent need pressing toward the same destination. We all hope to get *there*. There being a life that is shared. Even if we get there at different times through different doors.

SIX

By the Numbers

Is this lack of coupling and delayed childrearing a cross-cultural phenomenon or specific only to well-educated, financially secure, metropolitan professionals? Well, that's a very good question. I've been asking it myself during the many interviews I have had for this book. These meetings have taken place in coffee shops, libraries, diners and plush lobbies of upscale hotels. I have met in offices and apartments—some richly appointed, some decorated in early eBay and embellished only by a cat lounging on makeshift bookshelves across from a couple of Ikea chairs. Some of the women spend a considerable amount of their salary on upscale wardrobes and accessories and some barely have enough excess cash to shop H&M. A few party at topnotch bars with bottle service, a few kick back with a beer at home. A portion of the women interviewed are pursuing careers in the arts, and although some are Ivy League graduates, they scrape by waiting tables or use their considerable intellect to tutor so that they may keep their schedules flexible for auditions and still pay the rent. The one thing they all have in common is that they are extremely knowledgeable and articulate about the issue and for the most part, very well-educated.

Perhaps those who are more articulate are attracted to a study of this sort, but regardless, they have all thought long and hard about their—I want to call it a *predicament*, but by definition that confers negativity (predicament, noun: a difficult, unpleasant, or embarrassing situation). If I use that term, it connotes shame. It also suggests the ability to remove oneself from such a situation. I might be inclined to call it a plight, but that too, has a negative connotation. Maybe bind is a better, more neutral word, as being unmarried and childless near the end of a woman's fertility should not be deemed an "embarrassing situation." It *does*, however, tie them up in knots. Hence: a bind. That is, for those who *wish* to have children. Whatever we choose to call it, they are all stuck in this unpregnant pause between high fertility and menopause; no babies and little time.

But let's get right to it. My ladies have all been wonderfully open and giving, downright soul-bearing. They too, want answers. And when I tell you this is happening, I have the statistics to back it up. This phenomenon of women who want to be married and have children but haven't found a spouse—this unpregnant pause—is happening predominantly in large metropolitan areas. It is not happening at the same rate or with the same intensity in little towns from sea to shining sea.

I am not a statistician, I proclaim, by way of freeing myself from the stacks of numbers I never wanted to deal with during the high school math classes I continually cut in favor of hanging out in the chorus room. But I am grateful to those who do like to work the numbers for helping us see concrete patterns in things that we observe.

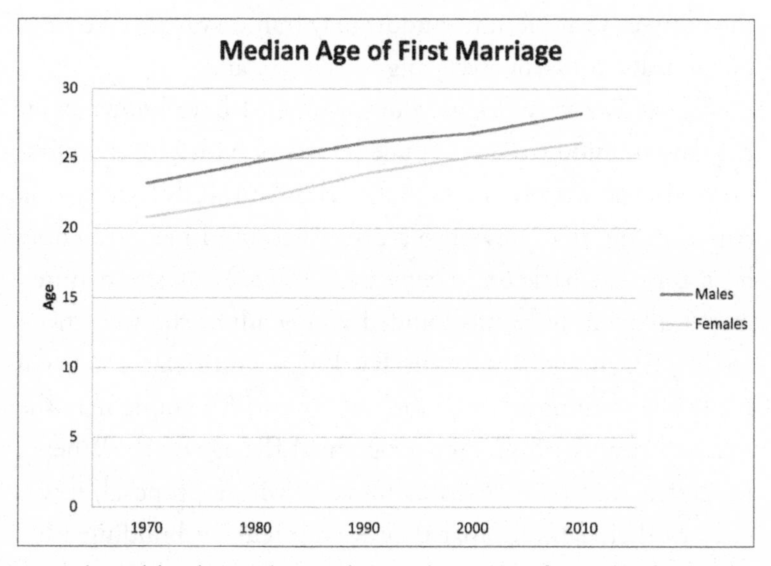

The table above shows the median age of men and women when they first marry in the United States covering the years from 1970 to 2010.[1] The median age for a man's first marriage was a ripe old 26.1 in 1990. The 2010 Census discovered it had crept up to 28.2 years. Likewise, the median age for a woman's first marriage was 26.1 years in 2010, up from 23.9 in 1990. Although this graph reflects national reporting, the statistics can be teased out from our informal survey of *The New York Times* "Vows" section, to show an even higher age for first marriages in New York City.

So ladies, you aren't getting any younger. As you gaze out the picture window of your dorm/apartment/parents' split level, staring at the campus quad/busy city/patch of backyard and contemplate your dream of becoming a doctor, you also need to think about how are you going to finish medical school, intern in Chicago, do that fabulous fellowship in San Diego and marry the man of your dreams before your fertility takes the plunge. That picture window may frame a dream-like view, but in reality, it's not a very big window at all.

Cassie is a very bright young woman I have known since her days in middle school. A talented actor with a lovely soprano voice, she was often cast in the school musicals I directed (a part-time gig that grew into a career because I had a teaching license to fall back on. *Thank you, Mama.*). As she matured into a diligent and well-rounded young adult, she went from an Ivy League college to an Ivy League medical school, all while maintaining an on-going romance with a young man she met at a summer SAT prep program at the age of 15. When a romantic vacation in Paris culminated with a proposal, it was clear to their families that they were intent on building a life together. But *when*? And *where*?

His job placed him in one city. Her school was located five hours away. They considered marrying during spring break, but that didn't leave enough time for a honeymoon. She chose a wedding dress during one weekend home, invitations on another. They planned their menu by Skype and finalized the guest list by email. They squeezed their nuptials into a three-week hiatus during Cassie's summer and fall session at medical school. It was a beautiful wedding. But no sooner had she changed out of her dress and moved her stuff into their temporary new home, she was back in class and he was commuting on weekends (or not, if she was too busy with labs to even see him).

She graduated and is now in rotations, considering specialties. She and her husband are currently in the same city, but that has a finite life (two months). The couple anticipates they will be living separately with Cassie's next assignment. By the time she finishes, she will be in her early thirties. Oops! That gives her only 5 years of prime fertility left at the very same time she is trying to establish her medical practice.

Sorry, Sheryl, if you are leaning into your career, you don't have time to lean into your husband.

But its okay! The statistics show the average age for first time mothers has also increased. So go. Do. Make your mark on the world. And if nature doesn't work, there are always the fertility folks. We know where they are.

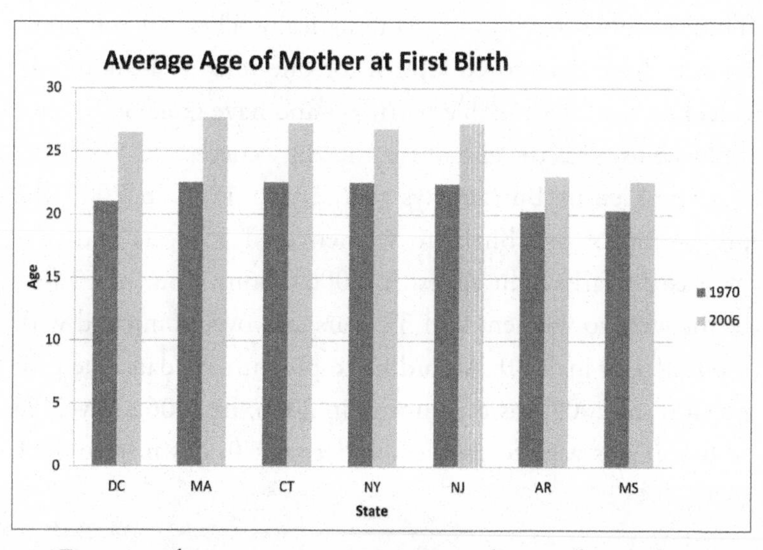

For me, there are two interesting things about the stats for first time motherhood. The first is that there is a significant difference among states.[2] In 1970, the average age of the mother at the birth of her first child was lowest in Arkansas (20.2 years) and highest in Connecticut, Massachusetts, and New York (22.5 years). Okay, not such a big deal—2 years. But by 2006, Massachusetts had the highest age at first birth (27.7 years) and Mississippi had the lowest (22.6 years), with New York not far behind at 26.8. What are women in Massachusetts and New York doing with those extra five years? Hmmm . . . medical school maybe?

This supports the argument that there is greater delay of marriage and subsequent childbearing in areas of higher density, states with big cities. And perhaps bigger dreams? Maybe that's why some of these women gravitated to the big city in the first place.

A really interesting statistic is that the greatest increase in women having babies is the population of women over 35. These numbers have gone up dramatically. These are the women who have delayed childbirth for one reason or another—career or lack of a suitable partner—and have gone on to have children towards the end of their fertility curve.

The Census Bureau says that, "from 1970 to 2006 the proportion of first births to women aged 35 years and over increased nearly eight times. In 2006, about 1 out of 12 first births were to women aged 35 years and over compared with 1 out of 100 in 1970. According to preliminary data, the proportion for 2007 was the same as in 2006. In 2006, only 21% of first births were to mothers under age 20, down from 36% in 1970.[3]

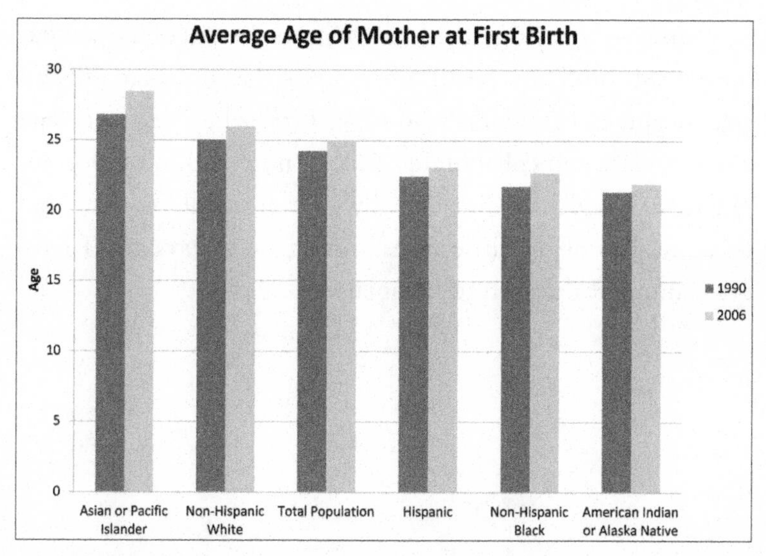

And lest you think this is a white metropolitan issue, the Census Bureau reports:

> Average age at first birth *increased for all racial and ethnic groups* between 1990 and 2006 with increases ranging from 0.6 years for American Indian or Alaska Native (AIAN) women to 1.7 years for Asian or Pacific Islander (API) women.
>
> In 2006, API women had the oldest average age at first birth (28.5 years), whereas AIAN women had the youngest (21.9 years); a difference of 6.6 years. The average age at first birth for non-Hispanic white women (26.0 years) was older than the average for the U.S. population (25.0 years) while those for non-Hispanic black (22.7 years) and Hispanic women (23.1 years) were younger (Figure 4).[4]

Suffice it to say that the United States Bureau of Census has done their job. I am specifically grateful that there are diligent statisticians in this world who make it *their* business to collate and correlate and collaborate so that I might whine about not having a grandchild and actually be statistically correct that there are less of the little tykes around these days and I have every numerical reason to complain.

SEVEN

Possibilities

Hold the presses! Damn the statistics! There is a sliver of hope on the horizon. My son tells me he and his wife are expecting a baby! She is in her waning fertility years and they have been anxious about conceiving. There has been much whispered talk over the past few months, but no declarations. It is rude to assume they have been trying and even ruder to ask. As eager as I am to be a grandmother, I know the line between concerned parent and intrusive mother-in-law. At least I claim to.

They are only seven weeks pregnant, but they let me in on their secret because they know how much I want this to happen. They are generous and want me to share their joy of anticipation. I fight the urge to drop whatever I am doing and go out to buy *Goodnight Moon*. I close my eyes and take a deep breath. I practice ujjayi breathing and I feel my pulse start to slow. I *can* contain myself. I must. It is early. Early, I caution.

But I hear it calling anyway. *Grandma*. It reverberates in my head and brings butterflies to my stomach. *Grandma*. I am carrying this news in a little pocket in my heart and it colors everything I do. At the grocery store I take a short detour through the diaper aisle on my way to produce. In Bloomingdale's for some concealer, I cruise through the layettes that are not remotely on the way to cosmetics. I chastise myself for spending too much time daydreaming.

Work and real life intersect. Being the neurotic I am, I go to the computer to look up the stats for healthy births in 35-year-old mothers. Maybe the Bureau of Census has some numbers that will lower my anxiety and help me pass the next seven-plus months of waiting for the next generation.

FAMILY FIRST

"Family first" is their motto. "We always had to eat dinner together and talk about our day," says Francine about growing up the youngest in a large Italian-American family. "We visited my grandmother's house every Sunday with all the relatives." This tradition now extends to her three children. Her son and his wife and children live in an adjacent property and her daughters have their own apartments. But they echo her sentiment.

"Family is the most important thing in life," says 34-year-old Jill.

"Family was always the most important thing in the world," repeats Lindsay, 30. "It was always assumed that I, too, would grow up to have a husband and children. We still talk about that as being in my future."

Francine remembers her home life as very happy. "My parents had a great marriage, they were very affectionate with each other . . . my mother was happy and social and enjoyed life to the fullest . . . and my dad was very family-oriented. He may not have played with us, but he enjoyed taking us places. We had many outings on the weekend like dinner in Chinatown or Little Italy."

"My mother did not work outside the house or drive a car . . . but she took in embroidery factory work that she did late at night to make some spending money that she didn't have to ask my dad for," Francine says. "She would advise us to have more independence, to have our own money." Francine worked as a teacher from the time her youngest child entered middle school.

Lindsay and Jill have very similar memories of their childhood. "[It was] the best of the best. [My mom] showed me a functioning, happy and loving marriage and a loving, supportive, functional family," says Lindsay. "She instilled in me that I should always feel very lucky to have my siblings and that if I ever needed anything, she and my father were there for me and would help me out of any situation."

Jill says of her mother, "She revolved her entire existence around her family, we did lots of activities together as a family. We went on vacations all together. We ALWAYS had dinner together with no distractions permitted. It was unacceptable to miss family dinners unless I gave ample notice that I had other plans . . . my mom always let us know that we were the most important and fulfilling aspect of her life. I remember her telling me when I was quite young that she had always wanted to be a mother and that she felt incredibly lucky to have had us and a husband she adored."

Both young women say their father is a very happy guy. "I never remember him complaining about work or anything else," says Jill.

"Being around his children, and now his grandchildren, make him the happiest," adds Lindsay.

It sounds idyllic. Only one of the daughters mentions that her parents "momentarily had a rough patch and a short separation." She believes "It was the best thing that ever happened to their relationship despite how hard it was in the moment." Fully invested in "Family First," neither Francine nor her other daughter felt it was relevant enough to include in their family history.

Lindsay thought that by this time in her life she would be married with kids and living in the suburbs, pursuing a career in performance. She is single, living in Brooklyn with a roommate and teaching music *(teaching! Not that I have anything against teaching . . . but).*

Jill confides that she really started thinking about herself as an adult around the age of 16. "I imagined I would travel the world working with some sort of charitable intentions. I had very vague ideas about the future. Throughout my late teens up until my mid-twenties I imagined my future adult self to be single, free of attachment, without children, working in anthropology or environmental activism, not making much money, but happy . . . I still wasn't sure about a husband or children. I thought marriage was simply unnecessary and too restrictive. I wasn't interested in having children because that life choice seemed more work and stress than it was worth."

Now she says "marriage makes sense to me. I want to have that ultimate commitment to one another, to be able to call ourselves a family . . . I've realized that I do not want to rely only on the relationship I have with my partner to fulfill me for the rest of my life. I want our family to be more than just the two of us. When my grandmother passed away a few years ago, I realized that I don't want to die alone, but rather, like her, surrounded by her children and grandchildren. I want children, but at this moment I don't feel ready. I wish the decision wasn't dictated by biology. I would wait ten more years if I felt safe in doing so, but I think its risky."

Lindsay also would like to have children. "I want to share my wonderful family with a new generation and continue this beautiful clan." And she would like to be in a relationship. "I think I can live a happy life without one, but I think I would be happier in one. I would also not want to have children on my own, so I would not do that unless I found a partner."

Jill and Lindsay both acknowledge that times have changed. "My mother got married young and subsequently was not in many other relationships before she got married," says Lindsay. "She grew up with my father since they have been together since they were 19 or 20, as opposed to me who has spent the first 29 years of my life dating different people and experiencing life with mostly friends or by myself . . . I am not sure I consciously chose this different path; I think life is just different now . . . I did however, definitely choose to end a serious relationship at the end of my college career because I did not want to end up feeling settled that young."

"My path has been 'windier,' than my mother's," observes Jill, "but now I want what she has . . . I know that I will need more in my life, outside of caring for my family to be happy and fulfilled. The opportunity to have an identity, and a life beyond my role as homemaker, has been created by feminist culture *(are you hearing this, Betty? Aren't you proud?)*. American women have become more than our roles, viewed by society as capable, whole significant individuals with voices, needs, and desires."

"Here lies the problem," says Francine, "Having told my girls to be independent, I would love nothing better than for them to have a husband and family."

The great irony of this family's structure is that although

they have chosen to live a communal life similar to generations of relatives before them, with shared resources and extended family in close proximity, the clan is not expanding as they expected. Only the son has married and produced grandchildren. The daughters, who received a clear message about the joys of motherhood and family, are eager to continue the strong family line, but are stuck in the unpregnant pause. They want to perpetuate beloved traditions, but they have no partners. They are left to wonder who will come when it is their turn to cook Sunday dinner.

I can't help but think this is so unfair. Biology be damned, Dr. Landsman.

EIGHT

Back to School

You might think having a pregnant daughter-in-law would cool my jets about the whole grandparenting pursuit, but it has not. I have *three* children. My youngest is still safe from his mother's grasp as he is only in his mid-twenties and newly engaged. But my daughter is creeping up to the fertility threshold. And she's happily ensconced in her life, not worrying about the impending doom awaiting her not-yet hard-boiled eggs. Call me greedy. Call me needy. Call me anything, but please: call me Grandma. I want to hear it everywhere. In the kitchen. On the phone. On my laptop. In the car. With green eggs and ham, and Sam-I-am, shouted near and far.

But you don't get to be a grandma without someone getting pregnant. And as I have discovered, getting pregnant these days is not so easy. And even when it is, there are delays. Women delay it for graduate school, for work, for travel. They delay it out of fear. They delay it because of biological ignorance. They delay it waiting for Mr. Right.

With all the choices presented to women today, I wonder what is being taught in schools. Is there an academic aspect to explore? I decide to seek out a woman's studies professor at a local college to see if she might shed some light on the topic.

Dr. Sarah Hosey is the Coordinator of the Women's Studies

Project and Assistant Professor in the Department of English at Nassau Community College. Like so many of the women I have spoken with, she is smart and beautiful. Her clear blue eyes are at once penetrating and kind. Her voice is musical, yet authoritative. I find myself feeling more than a bit of remorse for the lack of regard I gave my own professors in college. I was flip and argumentative. I had a big chip on my shoulder that I was daring someone, *anyone*, to try and knock off. I thought the world owed me an apology for where my zygote had landed. But sitting across the desk from this lovely person, I want nothing more than to apologize to *her* for the disrespect I had shown my teachers back then. All that information I missed trying to justify my right to be there!

She generously hands me the reading packet for Women's Studies 101. The first thing that catches my eye is a sidebar that declares there are 652 women's and gender studies programs at community colleges, four-year colleges, and universities in the United States.[1] That's probably about 650 more than when I started college in 1972. Back then I thought I was radical when I enrolled in Sol Gordon's seminal *(forgive the pun)* course Human Sexuality at Syracuse University during my sophomore year. I was sure I had learned everything I needed to know at the dining room table, working on my mother's class projects. Now, as I approach my sixth decade, I've become more comfortable discovering what I still don't know. And doing something about it.

The handout consists of photocopied pages from a textbook, reprints of articles from the online women's news site Jezebel, clippings from author Belle Hooks, a feminist and social activist who has published over 30 books, and the terrific

"Everything You Always Wanted to Know About Feminism But Were Afraid to Ask" by Rachel Fudge that appeared in the *Bitch Magazine* anniversary issue, published in 2005. It details every kind of feminism from suffrage to third wave in a way that is palatable to all political persuasions. It informs the dialogue on feminism. I think it should be required reading for everyone. So, stop for a moment. Jot down the web address and read what she has to say. It will change minds.[2]

Hosey also includes historical documents, creative literature and articles by and about men. "They have to be part of the dialogue," she says. "There is an assumption that feminists dislike men. Why do people make that intellectual leap, that advocating for women's rights and equal treatment and a more equitable world would be anti-male?"

We move quickly into our conversation about what is being taught and what is actually absorbed by her students. She recounts a conversation that she has heard before. "We are talking about work/life balance and I ask the students 'how are you going to do this?' And one student answers, 'I am going to finish college and start my career and then take time off when my kids are little, then go back to finish my career.' We are doing them a bit of a disservice when we don't talk frankly about the toll motherhood can take on your career and the toll that a career can take on your motherhood." These girls aren't even out of college and they are already trying to balance the desire for both family and meaningful work. Is it fair to tell them they may grapple with this dilemma for the rest of their fertile years?

Hosey says, "the notion that you can have a career—and we are not talking about a job here—that you care deeply about, that you want to be ambitious about and then want to suddenly take time off is a lie for many careers. In Academia and Law, these are the most productive years and the most fertile."

I pose my essential question to her: so did the Women's Movement sell us a bill of goods?

"I think the Women's Movement did a great job showing women and girls that there are other things besides motherhood. The Women's Movement did a great job of opening doors for us, and blazing the trail . . . but the world failed us. The world didn't keep up with the feminist movement."

To illustrate her point, she recounts an article she read about a woman who was arrested for neglect and child abandonment. The woman worked at McDonalds and had left her nine-year-old daughter who was home for summer vacation at a playground with a cell phone. The woman's defense was that it is hard to find a babysitter when you are making minimum wage.

The post-feminism individualism argument, explains Hosey, is that the woman should have taken responsibility for arranging some kind of childcare. That doesn't take into account "the extent that it is nearly impossible in this world to make both work. . . . It is more about how our capitalist society is structured than with the failure of feminism."

I ask her about the dichotomy between Patton's views and those of Sandberg: the need to lean in during a woman's most fertile years. "We generally don't value motherhood or parenting. We pay a lot of lip service to it and talk about how important it is, but our workplaces and our arts and our professional world are not structured to accommodate being a parent."

Is it changing? "I don't want to give too much away to

the idea that once you have women in leadership positions, they will automatically do the right thing . . . we need women to speak up, whether they are in positions of power or students." Sandberg is a good example, she says. When she was 8 ½ months pregnant, she didn't blame men for not having special parking for expectant women at Google. No one had asked for it before.

"Do we need pregnancy parking on this campus? Probably," Hosey says. "Places for students to nurse [a baby] on campus? Absolutely. If she was in a position of power to get those things done for her sisters . . . " The sentence hangs unfinished in the air. Sandberg got those spaces for the women at Google. Who will advocate at Nassau Community College? Activism matters.

"I think these things are changing as we have these conversations," muses Hosey." We are making progress in that women are making demands and advocating for change."

We talk a little about the delay of childrearing as a movement and Hosey echoes the sentiment of the early feminists. "I come back to trusting women to make the right choice for themselves. I don't see a downside to self-actualization."

She says she, herself, saw two choices growing up. "One model was the beleaguered housewife who does everything for her husband. She references *Of Woman Born*, by Adrienne Rich who died in 2012. "And the other was the image of the liberated women offered to me by the Women's Movement."

I was not familiar with Rich's work but thought I should be. Thank you, Google. "The primary thesis of Rich's book is that motherhood is both the private reality that women experience as mothers and the social institution of motherhood that limits women to their nurturing role," writes MD Brady on her blog. "In the 1970s, no one had paid serious attention to motherhood, beyond sentimental praise or mother blaming. Many of us were rebelling against the lives we saw our mothers living, especially those of us in the white middle-classes. We were matriphobic, fearing we would become our mothers."[3]

Now we spend more time naval gazing—at our own and our children's—and theories of how to successfully combine family and career abound.

"I made a clear choice when I was in my twenties," Hosey says. "I didn't want to do dishes or keep house or do other people's laundry—well, I *do* do other people's laundry; I have two kids. I am in an equitable relationship that I feel I had to carefully negotiate for, and I have the Women's Movement to thank for that."

The students in Hosey's classes feel the empowerment brought by the Women's Movement as well. "But their idea of empowerment is a little bit superficial. They think 'I can have sex with whomever I want, it's my business . . . and I can do whatever I want in terms of my career' They don't suffer from the illusion that they are going to be working at Google, but the message of *Lean In* is empowering."

Hosey's students know something is not quite right "when it comes to gender in this world. They are not tapped into the bigger problems and they haven't had to articulate them in any meaningful way. A lot of this stuff is brand new, but when they saw Beyonce[4] on the [2014] Video Music Awards holding up a feminist sign, it was very exciting to their minds."

Despite all the enlightenment surrounding us, bouncing off our cultural icons and reflected back from our televisions, there is a long way to go yet. Hosey was pulled aside after class by the mother of a student who asked if her daughter would still be able to find a husband if she "goes into this stuff." When she asks her class what people say about them taking this course, the answers are archaic. "My boyfriend asked if taking this class would make me a man-hating feminist," one student reported.

"That's a pretty standard reaction. I usually say, tell them: I am a grown woman and taking one class is not going to turn me into something I don't want to be. I think there is still something a little frightening about the term 'feminist' because the women think it will alienate the men around them."

When Hosey first meets her class she asks who in the class is a parent and then follows it up with the question of who would like to be. "Nobody has ever asked them that before," she says. "That's the assumption, the family model. We don't ask men if they are going to have kids the same way we ask women." She does the same thing with marriage but adds the question "Do you want to marry someone of the same gender?" The times and attitudes are changing.

"It is important to have these conversations not just with our girlfriends and our mothers, but in public spaces, in forums that also include men . . . we need them as our allies. The work is ongoing. Girls feel like they can be president. This is stage one—just getting us into these positions. Maybe stage two will be grappling with these issues, what it means for our biological lives."

Hosey is proud of what the feminists have accomplished and doesn't see a backlash. "I don't blame feminism. I applaud feminism. I blame capitalism more. I am seeing calls for universal childcare . . . we are starting to recognize that someone has to watch the kids. Attention is being paid." Finally.

I am invigorated by my conversation with Hosey. I feel there might be a successful way to synthesize a woman's desire for a family and her need for outside achievement. Maybe Sheryl Sandberg and Susan Patton could sit down to tea, agree to disagree about the timeline, but put their heads together and write some awesome legislation that would make it possible for young women to really have it all. It will also be interesting to see how and if Sandberg's position changes in light of her recent widowhood.

AN AMERICAN DREAM

Ruth is 66. Her daughter Lia is 30. They live in San Diego. Ruth has been in a loving marriage to Sam, Lia's father, for 37 years. Lia, a self-supporting manager at an educational non-profit company, lives alone. She is the only one of their three daughters not married. Is this distressing to Ruth? Not terribly. "Although I would like to see her have a significant other," she says, "ultimately that is her decision."

Lia, also, is not freaking out about her single status. "I would like to be in a relationship, but feel that I am supported in other aspects of my life—family, friends, career—so [I] am able to live a happy life without being in a relationship."

Ruth and Sam were in their late 30's when they had Lia and her twin sister. They are well educated and financially comfortable. Sam was an attorney and Ruth has a master's in education. What is different about Ruth, though, from the other mothers I have interviewed is that she is a child of Holocaust survivors. Her mother lost most of her family during the war.

Ruth tells her story. "My parents married in 1942 in the Jewish ghetto of my mother's hometown in Poland. After becoming separated and sent to endure various concentration camps, they miraculously found each other in Austria after World War II. They both wanted to leave Europe to start anew." Ruth was born in the Displaced Persons Hospital in Linz, Austria. "Two years later, we all emigrated to San Diego. I think my parents always felt blessed to have found each other."

Her mother was always "a little anxious and haunted by her experiences" and her father had a "stoic attitude but also a great sense of humor. I think he was happy to be in America." They became U.S. citizens as soon as they were able. Her father worked hard to support the family, striving for "the comfort of the American Dream." Although he worked long hours, he was usually home for dinner. "I remember watching the evening news and television shows with him," says Ruth.

Lia grew up thinking she would get married, have children, and pursue a successful career, although she does not recall Ruth *telling* her that this was the path. She saw her mother return to teaching when she was eight years old. "I believe it was by choice [but] later by necessity to allow us to attend our school as out-of-district students." The girls then went on to private colleges in the East, which Ruth believes "made them more independent."

Ruth may not have had a heart-to-heart sit down with her daughters to lay out a plan, but she did model her values. She taught Lia about "setting boundaries, being firm (yet still loving); not giving your child whatever they want, but enough to be happy." Her message was "trust your children and allow them to flourish rather than being too involved and demanding; stress the importance of education and doing well in school."

Her father made sure they learned to "place family as first priority" then to choose your career by "what you enjoy vs.

money." He discouraged the girls from becoming lawyers because "he didn't like being one, even though it's a lucrative career," Lia says.

"I feel that sometimes people pity me for being single at 29, but I am confident enough in what I am looking for in a boyfriend that I am not willing to lower my standards or settle just for the sake of being in a relationship. I do feel that my lower need for a significant other stems from my family upbringing and my parents' insistence that I do what makes me happy, not what society says is right . . . if I wanted to have a boyfriend today, it wouldn't be hard to find someone that wants to date me. Instead, I'm holding out to find a boy that makes me happy, shares my interests/values/sense of humor, someone that I'm excited about and want to spend all my time with and I'd rather be single until I find this type of guy . . . while I would like to become a mother (and eventually a grandmother), it is not the most important thing in the world to me. I believe my life would still be complete and happy without children," says Lia.

"My mother got married at 29, which I am not on track to do. I also think the world in which we live today is different than my mother's in that it's more acceptable by society to not get married and have children. Perhaps if I was growing up during my mom's time, I would feel a stronger urgency."

I am moved by this young woman. Her confidence is admirable and her positive outlook, inspiring. I would like to check in on her in seven or eight years and see how she is doing. She may be content right now, but I'm worried by what Dr. Keefe might have to say about her aging eggs. I am afraid that Dr. Thompson would tell her she's already pushing past the season for the big freeze.

It's a pressure these young women do not need and should not have, but they do. I want to say: let them be happy. Let them work and play at their own speed. Whatever happens, happens. Qué será, será! But that is not the world we live in. Instead, I think: let them not have regrets.

NINE

The Psychologists

Okay, so I have gone to the doctors and I have gone back to school. I get the drive to have children before the eggs go bad. Of course I do. I am as weepy and wanting as many of the women I have interviewed. I am embarrassed to say I am practically a one-woman cheering squad for having babies. Lots of them. And now that I have a cursory understanding about the biological imperative to freeze those eggs while they are still good, I feel that I am still missing a crucial part of the picture. And that is the psychological profile.

As a former drama teacher who worked with adolescents for over 20 years, I learned that no two people fit into the same box; the majority of people hardly fit into boxes at all. We would need large, odd shaped baggies to contain all the various shapes and sizes of people we meet in the course of a lifetime. We are all products of vastly different backgrounds and experiences, but for the sake of research it is necessary to find the similarities that can be grouped together to suggest a trend or a pattern. These are the elements I sought to discover from the psychologists.

Before I introduce my esteemed panel of experts, it is important to point out that these doctors work with women who have elected to pursue fertility treatment or have individually sought out a therapist. Their sampling may or may not reflect the feelings of those countless other women who move forward in their lives without a partner or child, who can't afford or don't chose fertility clinics, therapists or years of introspection. But I feel hearing from the psychologists is crucial to understand the issue. So let's begin.

I trek to a part of New Jersey where I am unfamiliar with the roads. My navigation takes me around one jug-handle after another (a delightful Jersey highway specialty) and I begin to surmise that I am going in circles. I stop the car and get my bearings. I use my head and my innate good sense of direction, realizing it is better to follow my gut rather than the pompous woman in the dashboard. I make note to remember this; it is a good life lesson.

I arrive with time to spare before meeting Dr. Claudia Pascale, Director of Psychological and Support Services at the Institute for Reproductive Medicine and Science at Saint Barnabas Medical Center in Livingston, NJ. As a psychologist and member of the treatment team at IRMS, she oversees a myriad of educational services designed to help patients cope with the emotional, psychological and ethical dilemmas of infertility.

I find Dr. Vivian Diller through an online article she has written. She is an oft-quoted psychologist in private practice in New York City working with adults, adolescents and couples in long and short-term therapy and graciously agrees to talk with me by phone. She wrote the book *Face It: What Women Really Feel as Their Looks Change*, and is a regular contributor to online blogs, as well as the *Huffington Post* and *Psychology Today*. Diller appears regularly on television and radio as a commentator on psychological, family and lifestyle issues.

With help once again from my good buddy nurse Nancy Amsel *(I owe you more than lunch, girlfriend)*, I meet Dr. Shelley Lee, the Director of Psychological Services at the NYU Fertility

Center. She is a clinical psychologist with extensive experience working with individuals and couples undergoing infertility treatment. Her private practice also includes clients with psychological issues unrelated to infertility.

Although I speak with each of these experts separately, I have grouped them into one chapter as they are all addressing the same topic, albeit from different angles: the American Dream of growing up, getting married and having kids.

"We missed a big piece," says Lee of the Women's Movement. "I see women every day who come to this clinic for donor sperm, and in some way they had this dream . . . [they] are grieving the fact that they always expected to be moms and married. And all they have to hold on to is the idea of being moms through donor sperm . . . they are very tearful if they are in their early forties as they realize their chance is 15%, and they can't let go . . . they have lost the husband, the family and the possibility of their own eggs."

Diller says, "That delay [caused by] making room for careers has created the boom in fertility centers. The urge to parent is especially strong in women who feel that [their fertility] is going. They have this panicky feeling that 'I won't have this chance again.'" But she cautions that "It is easy to see it as women who are victimized because they have a time clock running out; they are fearful they will be overlooked. But it is a sociological phenomenon. Marriage itself is changing. Women are involved in their careers and have missed the boat."

Lee recounts the story of one of her clients, a 42-year-old woman who grew up in a traditional family. Her sister got married early and had three children. Lee's client was an adventurer. She used her twenties and thirties to travel the world, but now is sitting in Lee's office trying to figure out if motherhood is still a possibility.

"I meet a lot of successful women who are the ones who have the most difficulty with the fertility process," says Pascale. "It's something they can't control . . . it's their bodies taking over. They made a decision to put their house in order, whether it's their career or their environment. They wanted the house, they wanted to be secure, but in the process of doing that, they weren't aware of putting their fertility on hold. The problem is sometimes you never know when age is going to get you. You never know if you are going to have [fertility] problems."

So much of the disappointment has to do with unmet expectations. Many of the women profiled here grew up with the assumption they would marry and start a family. That was a given. The career aspect was the exciting, unknown part. They became explorers and adventurers in the new world of opportunity and choice.

"Choice!" exclaims Pascale, who is preparing a paper on the topic for a symposium, "We thought choice would make us happier. It has made us unhappier. With all the electronic dating services, you don't meet the guy next door."

"For single women," says Lee, "It is not easy when they have had very clear expectations for many, many years that they were going to have the nuclear family."

One of my interviewees, Elizabeth, who you will meet shortly, sees a larger picture. She thinks the system of marriage as a whole is crumbling and I ask the professionals if they believe this to be true.

"Women's lives were so different in the 1940s and '50s," explains Lee. "They didn't work. They were dependent on husbands. You built your house, took your vacation. There was not a big voice for women at that time."

"Women in their thirties look at the storybook image of marriage," says Diller. "But the reality is they looked at marriages that weren't good. Culture is not good to marriage. You can have sex without being married; it's no longer a necessary institution. Its option quality has made women realize it may not happen. [The] focus on partnering has changed to looking for someone who might be good to have a family with. They are thinking practically. Not just about love—but what you want in life.

Diller continues, "I think the *idea* of marriage used to be more about a contract between two people to share the roles, that in marriage, a traditional marriage, happiness wasn't necessarily part of the contract. The notion that when you meet someone you will be happy is relatively new in the 20th century. It has guided women away from traditional marriage, [and the idea] that it will give them happiness. Falling in love is the early stage. Then, are you compatible? There is this misguided idea that marriage will bring you happiness."

"What's crumbling," observes Lee about contemporary marriage, "Is the one-way-to-go system . . . when [women] first learn it is not happening the way they thought, there is overwhelming grief and mourning. When they get used to it, there is a value shift. And although it is not what they expected, the acceptance comes and it is an important part of moving forward."

"The Women's Movement gave women a voice to follow their interest and career," Lee says. "They gained position, power and money and [the freedom] to feel like you are self-determining. These are important things, important for all women. But the piece about motherhood and family was dropped along the way. The women I see always had the fantasy of husband and kids. Or, if it wasn't dropped, time goes by so quickly and careers are consuming, lots and lots of hours with not a lot of social life."

But all is not lost. There are many ways to have a child within and without the fertility centers (we haven't even touched on surrogates or adoption). Pascale recounts a recent presentation she attended where a lesbian psychiatrist gave a talk about families. "She talked about this spreadsheet developed by her 12-year-old daughter, who started counting the ways we can create family. 'There are 31,' she said." And that's good news.

SISTER ACT

"I made very different choices and mistakes than my mom," says 31-year-old Doreen. "I also learned from hers . . . but I feel I went a little further in the sense that I was able to go to school and travel and be 'free' because I chose not to have children. I feel like I am running from the whole marriage and family thing because of . . . my family. I don't want to have children that turn out like me and the way I think, [should they] have to deal with divorce like I did. I don't want to be stuck and miserable like a lot of people."

"I always wanted kids since I was little," says Colleen, Doreen's big sister by two years. "I wanted to nurture and take care of someone. I had this biological urge." She tried to have children during her brief marriage at the age of 25, but her husband had a low libido and testosterone issues. "He was more interested in the computer than me." They divorced after seven years of marriage, with Colleen leaving her husband for her high school sweetheart. That lasted less than a year.

"I casually dated—I can meet men," she laughs, "but not necessarily the right men." She recognizes that even though she saw herself as independent, she was still catering to the men in her life. "It was always on their terms. I was always trying to reconcile my relationship with my father through the people I was dating. My father was always on a pedestal. He was distant. He didn't talk."

She looks back on it now through the self-knowledge gained in therapy and years of introspection. "It was textbook: I knew what was happening, but I did it anyway. It was the fear of being alone. I didn't want to be without sex. I was like a 17-year-old boy let loose out of school. It was ridiculous."

Doreen saw their father from another angle, as often happens with siblings in different places in the birth order. We all grow up in a somewhat different family, depending on where our family is emotionally and financially at the time we enter it. "I feel my father tried his hardest to be as physically and emotionally present as he could . . . I think he has a hard time being emotionally present in general. He was always affectionate, but I feel he shuts down when people get emotional . . . my father did everything he could do for his family. He instilled an incredible work ethic in me. Taking care of people you love is important. Family is important and you do whatever you can for them . . . he never made me feel pressured to be someone I am not. He always said 'do what makes you happy, be who you are.'"

Colleen and Doreen's parents divorced when the girls were seven and five. They lived with their mother until Colleen entered middle school, when they moved to their father's home. He remarried the following year.

"They had been together for many years," Colleen says of her father and stepmother. "My mother believed they were having an affair but my father said no. But I was okay with living with my father, I didn't get along with my mother and my mother didn't fight for us. She wanted us, but couldn't manage on her own, and I was becoming a difficult preteen." Her stepmother is an "independent woman onto herself. An independent, overbearing alcoholic. Money driven. We grew up in a household where everyone had to make money. She wanted the kids to make money so my father didn't have to support us. 'You support yourself at a certain stage,' She wasn't nurturing."

"Me and my stepmother get along," says Doreen, "but there is distance there. I feel like I always put a little distance between me and anyone . . . I have so much respect for my mom and stepmom but maybe if I hadn't grown up with my stepmom, who is an alcoholic, I wouldn't have thought drugs and alcohol were okay . . . I never want to put the blame on anyone else for how I behave . . . I don't like to say, yeah, if things were different, I would have been different, but yeah, maybe they could have been."

For the most part, the girls maintained good relations with their mother, who never remarried. "We were close when I was little," Doreen remembers. "But there was a lot both of us were dealing with and we should have been closer."

Their mother had been an actor and singer in her youth and encouraged Colleen to choose a career in performance. "She pushed me to pursue it when I was in high school," Colleen says. "I thought she was a little jealous when I was growing up and performing. I think she still wanted the spotlight."

When Colleen got married, she did the whole wedding

shmear. Poufy white dress. Limo. The Works. The week before the wedding, Colleen was crying and thinking about not going through with it. "My mother was on her knees begging me not to do it." Her father told her she could get out when they were in the limo on the way to the church. But not everyone listens to their parents, particularly ones we don't think have done such a swell job in their own lives.

Doreen did, though. She says her mother drove the point home. "DO NOT RUSH! WAIT UNTIL YOU'RE READY. BE INDEPENDENT!" She told her to find what makes her happy and be able to take care of herself first. Doreen says "She told me 'If you want to get married and are genuinely happy and secure in your relationship and yourself, then go for the kids. But kids are not easy to deal with. It's not a necessity, but it's a beautiful thing when the time is right.' She would always make sure I knew that having kids and getting married is not the only thing we have to do as women. It doesn't define us."

After a series of difficult and abusive relationships, Doreen is currently enjoying her independence. She recently completed a degree in a specialized medical technology and although she would like to be in a loving relationship, she is ambivalent about motherhood. "I do want to become a mother ONLY to teach my children how to love and respect not only other people, but themselves as well. I would want to raise all boys to teach them how to treat a woman, [or] I would want a girl to teach her how to treat herself and not settle for being treated any way other than what she deserves. I would want to teach them to stick up for themselves and not to be in love with money, to let go of fear and ego. I want to teach them to be genuinely happy and learn not to depend on material things and fake happiness." She has thought a lot about the responsibilities of parenthood, deeply influenced by her own upbringing.

"But," she adds, with frightening ambivalence, "I DON'T want to have kids because I am afraid they will do some of the bad things I did. I do not want them to make mistakes they can't take back. I don't want them to hate themselves."

Despite the difficulties of her upbringing and witnessing her sister's failed marriage, Doreen is a believer. "I think everyone should be in a relationship . . . we are human and need connection. It's extremely important to find a healthy relationship both mentally and physically. It helps us evolve." She tells me that although she had a hard time finding herself when she first became an adult, she has learned a lot. "It took me a long time to realize its okay to be single and sober. Haha," she scoffs. "But I have actually found my niche and have done amazingly well in school. I've never been happier."

But her sister is still seeking. "It has changed for me," says Colleen. "I have more of a drive to mother myself right now. I am more worried about what I want *my* life to be." Although she is in a relationship with a much older man, she has quit her job in New York City and is off to Ireland for a second master's degree. "I'm having a harder time making a commitment."

I ask her what the future would look like if she could script it. "I would find a husband my age in Ireland, have an amazingly healthy and fun relationship, and have black-haired, blue-eyed babies with brogues. I would have a wildly successful career traveling, and he would be home to take care of the kids. Part of me wants to be home with kids, but I *always* want to be able to do my thing."

The dream doesn't change. We all want to have it all.

TEN

How's Your Daddy?

Did you have a good one or a bad one? Somewhere in between? Can I really get away with blaming this failure to couple on mothers? That would be so easy. So *Freudian*. Back in the day when it took only *two* people to make a baby (as opposed to a whole team of fertility experts), one of those people was the father. And his influence in shaping our young women can't be dismissed, even though there are many women who seem to be doing a fine job of raising happy, well-adjusted children without a father present (check out singlemothersbychoice.org. *More on them later*).

Dr. Meg Meeker, author of *Strong Fathers, Strong Daughters*, opens her book with a stirring call to arms. "Men, good men: We need you . . . your daughter needs the best of who you are: your strength, your courage, your intelligence and your fearlessness. She needs your empathy, assertiveness and self-confidence. She needs *you*."

Her book makes a strong case for the power of the father/daughter relationship and how it carries over into the male/female dating dynamic:

> Our daughters need the support that only fathers can provide. When you come into a room, they change. Everything about them changes: their eyes, their

> mouths, their gestures, their body language. Daughters are never lukewarm in the presence of their fathers . . . they light up—or they cry.[1]

Those last two words hit me hard. A father can make it or break it. I know this to be true in my own life. I was not one of the lucky ones. I was not encouraged. I was not complimented. I was slapped on the ass and told I was fat. I was told that an education would be wasted on me, since I would grow up, get married and have babies. I was told, rather directly, that I was not valued in the way my brother was.

I remember my father encouraging my older brother to go after girls, reveling in his conquests. And I remember the night he caught me making out with my boyfriend of two years in his old Pontiac Star Chief. I was a senior in high school. I came into the house at curfew. My father sat waiting for me in his big easy chair with the matching ottoman. He called me a slut and demanded I terminate the relationship immediately. He didn't like this boy and he wouldn't tolerate my behavior. I argued. I cried. But I didn't break up with him. I just became a very good liar.

I spent a good part of the first half of my life (and countless dollars) on a therapist's couch trying to reconcile my father's meanness and rejection (quick synopsis: *he was mostly mad at my mother's blatant indiscretions and his sister's contempt and disdain for him, but being a woman as well, it spilled over onto me*).

My daughter, on the other hand, has had a great dad. He read to her from infancy, encouraged her at the piano, coached her soccer teams, provided musical accompaniment when she sang at talent shows. He told her she was smart, capable, *worthy*. He applauded her successes and was supportive when she made mistakes. Even when her marriage to that deceitful cocaine addict came to a dramatic end *(am I bitter? Yes!)*, he was there to pick up the pieces and the lawyer's bill. Was there something more he could have done that would have prevented her from being seduced by such a man? I don't know. But as a good dad, he was there to hold her and comfort her, redirect her energies and now they share a thriving business practice in the financial community. Can we save our children from every disappointment? I think not. But try, we will.

The afterword in Meeker's book could serve as a primer for fathers. The section headings are guideposts: "Realize Who You Are to Her," "Open Your Eyes to Her World (It's Different from Yours)," "Fight For Her Body," "Fight For Her Mind," "Fight For Her Soul."[2] What better advice could a father want? Wouldn't it be great if all men fathered in this manner?

Dr. Thompson, whom you met earlier, was one of the lucky ones. Remember: she came by her career naturally. Her father is also an obstetrician. "I think my dad dealing exclusively with women in his practice [was] an influence for us to be empowered," Thompson reflects. Raised in North Carolina, along with a younger sister who is now an attorney on Capitol Hill in Washington DC, she comes from a long line of professionals. Her parents left Jamaica to attend college in the United States and always put education at the forefront of their parenting.

"They sent us to the best schools. We were expected to do well. One semester I didn't make the dean's list and there was major drama." Thompson laughs about this now. "Both our parents wanted us to be independent and have our own careers but didn't want us to sacrifice our own families. Dad used to say MD before MRS."

Although her mother, a conservative woman from the West Indies, didn't talk much about the women's movement, she was involved with the Civil Rights Movement. As a teacher, she always had "an underlying thing about us having our own careers," Thompson says. She encouraged the girls to "hang out their own shingle" which meant law, medicine or business. "Whatever you choose, do it to the maximum degree," she told them.

"I think for my dad, it was more about understanding women's experiences through his profession. He wanted us not to go through some of the things he saw woman dealing with. I was more of a daddy's girl. I did more boy-like things with him, like going to [sporting] games. I don't think he missed having a boy. And I think he led by example. I chose medicine because I was exposed to it. I saw how happy he was . . . And this specialty has very few emergencies, so it melds nicely with having a family."

Thompson's husband Sean is an orthopedic surgeon and she muses on how times have changed. "I think my mom regretted not going to graduate school. She spent a lot of her twenties and thirties helping my father set up his practice. The people I grew up with, everyone was a professional and the wives worked in the offices. Even though the women were all educated, they didn't necessarily have the advanced degree . . . I would have liked to help Sean start his own practice, but I was a fellow at the time and had kids. I understand that sentiment of wanting to help him."

Danny Martin is also a hands-on father who values education. The father of three daughters, he has been intimately involved in their lives. "It was about encouragement, targets and goal-setting when the girls were young." He chuckles about the advertisements we grew up with in the '50s and '60s. "Clearly, there was a time that the majority of goal setting for women was mostly being a success at being a wife and mother [and] I have spent absolutely *no* time talking to my girls about this. There has been no discussion in our household about the skill sets required for wife and mother. There *is* a lot about the value of family being a good thing . . . one of the things that *is* different in this more modern era is working mothers [who] automatically, intrinsically provide the role model and illustration that there is value in both. You can do both and there is personal accomplishment in both."

He speaks passionately about his daughters and their successes. He has raised an attorney, a grad student pursuing a PhD in psychology and an artist working in the fashion industry. "My role has been to dream big and encourage them to make the most of themselves that they can make. That isn't intended to be to the exclusion of the joys of family or being a mother . . . my kids are accomplished, but I want them to reach for grander things."

Professional accomplishment is a big thing for Danny. Both he and his wife have successful careers in sales, but he looks around and sees a family full of professionals who are enjoying greater financial success. "The people who make it are the people who are highly focused and work narrowly toward a goal and take calculated steps, calculated internships, calculated jobs all designed to get to something they are very specifically aiming for. It's basically not a surprise when they get there. But you have to aim high enough. I keep nudging them to look higher up the ladder."

I ask him if he has imparted the same zeal to his girls about pursuing a personal life. "No," he says. "I don't think that is the job of a boy or a girl during college. I am actually happy to hear that my kids are in the library. I am happy when they have determined that this Thursday or this weekend is better spent *not* out drinking. They have better things to accomplish. You can't get to the places I am hoping for, or aiming for them to get to by going out three nights a week with your friends."

But Danny, I say, what about dating? What about boys? Don't you want them to get married and make you a grandpa? "If you pursue the activity you like to pursue, you will meet people who like to do what you like to do. College is the great meeting ground of all time but none of them truly understand that while it's going on." I fill him in on Princeton Mom. "I think that's accurate . . . but it sure as heck is not what I want for *my* girls!"

I badger him some more. Do you ever give the girls dating advice? He looks at me like I am a little crazy. Like maybe I haven't been listening or am stuck in some 1950s teen movie. "I can't ever recall advising or even discussing that subject. Their mother pushes a bit harder on putting yourself out there, going to better places and meeting a better class of guys . . . she says 'you need to be rubbing elbows with the kind of guys you want to meet.' I am quite certain that underlying it all, I have spent much more time talking to them about making themselves into someone they want to be. I don't think any of my daughters have any image that is built around the fact that the man they meet is going to make their life into what it is. Their image is that they have to make it happen and that the man is going to be an equal partner."

This brings me back to Dr. Larry Landsman. Also the

father of three girls, his "potent females," an older singlet and twins, are 22 months apart. The oldest of four boys, all engineers but him, he states emphatically that he did not want sons. "I wouldn't have it any other way," he says.

Like Danny Martin, he has been intimately involved with their upbringing. "I was there more than my wife when the girls were growing up. I have much more freedom than she does. I viewed being there for teenagers as much more important than infants." Since his daughters often saw Landsman in the lab, they all started out wanting to be doctors. His oldest daughter, Marcy, 31, holds a PhD in organic chemistry. His twins are both artists, one working in London the other in California.

"The fact that we had the twins [so close together] meant we needed our older daughter to take care of herself more. It had an impact on her independence and sense of self. She has made many more friends, deep close relationships through high school and college. The twins bonded in a way we can't understand. Our older girl was also overweight in college. Being overweight is one of the worst things that can happen to a girl in our society," says Landsman *(what a deeply upsetting thought)*.

This opinion reflects his position on how women attract mates. In accordance with the biological theory he put forth earlier: it is the man who chooses the woman, if the woman is overweight and not at her most attractive, she will not attract the man who might choose her for a mate. "This has affected Marcy's self-esteem, as she sees her friends getting married and having children." He believes it has influenced her previous choice of partners. "She met a guy who seemed fine from the outside. He never went to college, was working in IT, sleeping with other women during the relationship. He had no strong father figure. She settles for this guy and we open our home to him. She finally realizes this is unacceptable."

Larry looks like he could strangle the guy. I know that face. It was the murderous look my own husband had when he uncovered the arrest record for our daughter's ex. Sometimes it doesn't matter how great a dad you are, how many recitals you sit through, how many games you coach. Sometimes your brilliant, accomplished, beautiful child just falls in love with the wrong guy.

Hold on: I've been too delicate here. Let me rephrase that: sometimes your daughter *(or mine)* falls in love with a piece of shit. And it's not your fault. But, if you wait for it, mine will chime in later and may just explain how that might come to be.

ELEVEN

Let's Hear It from the Men

When I first began this project I had no intention of including anything about men except in relation to the women I was interviewing. I had relegated their gender to the role of "Dad" for this endeavor. But after speaking to my first dozen women, it became abundantly evident that there was no way to write this book fairly without hearing from a few men. So off I went to pillage my sons' address books *(thank you, boys!)* to see how the male counterpart fit into my lament. May I interject a resounding "Wow" at this juncture? WOW!

Was I naïve! *Of course* our young women are not acting in a vacuum of only women and women's evolution. Although they may still be the only ones *using* it. *Groan*. This is definitely a joint problem, a seesaw of the sexes, with women currently on the ascent.

Michael Kimmel writes in *Guyland: The Perilous World Where Boys Become Men*:

> The entry of overwhelming numbers of middle-class women in the workplace is largely responsible for the postponement of marriage and childrearing for both sexes. Today, with women appearing to be every bit as professionally competent career-oriented, and ambitious as men *[appearing to be?? Hey Kimmel!!]*, and equally capable of earning a

living wage, there is no longer the same sense of urgency for men to move toward 'getting a good job' to eventually provide for the marital needs of a wife and child."[1]

So if (some) men are no longer driven to make a gazillion dollars to give their families a life of luxury, and women can now be artificially inseminated as well as do the jobs men have been doing, why would women need to find a man at all? If they are not looking for someone to provide for them financially, then what *are* they looking for that can't be found among their fathers, brothers, straight and gay male friends?

At the risk of speaking for womanhood at large, which is more than a bit presumptuous, I think women are looking for LOVE. It's not something quantifiable or qualitative. It is amorphous and ethereal. And I don't think it has changed all that much with the generations. When the need for physical and financial protection is taken off the table, what remains is an intangible. It is the stuff of art and poetry. Partnership and companionship, yes, but there is more. They are searching for connection. And engagement. And intimacy. And maybe, just maybe, a little romance.

If this is true *(and being the hopeless romantic that I am, I believe it is)*, it behooves the argument to then ask: what are *men* looking for? My next interview is eye-opening; it makes me refocus my view of men. It forces me to abandon my assumptions and allow the nature vs. nurture argument to resurface. I have to consider that men and women are not looking for the same thing, that maybe they are not even in the same conversation. I have to once again examine the biological imperative of the caveman because, according to John Stonehill, author of the dating blog ChecktheirFridge.com, what men really want is for a woman to "Let the Dude Be the Dude" *(not that he's a real authority, but he has some interesting stuff to say).*

I meet with John on a gorgeous afternoon in a swanky hotel bar on the Upper East Side of Manhattan. I am early for our appointment. As I situate myself at a table with super delicious upscale nuts and my requisite cup of tea, I take in the surroundings. I don't think I have ever seen as many bespoke suits in one room. The men are of many nationalities; I hear languages I can't identify. But they are all uniformly, meticulously groomed. They are elegant. They are refined. But they are all peacocks, strutting from bar to lobby, tugging at their French cuffs, running fingers through their hair, or what is left of it. They scroll and troll their cellphones, peer into their laptops. They are in charge. They are the pride of the pride of Lions of Commerce. They are Very Important Dudes (VIDs). I decide that "Dudeness" has to be included when I speak with my male subjects.

ChecktheirFridge.com is a *(raise eyebrows, insert throat-clearing noise)* unique approach to dating for both men and women, gay or straight. "We are all dating detectives and we are all looking for something specific," says Stonehill, a tall, nice looking, somewhat frenetic guy in his early forties. "When we were growing up, we all came home from school and the first thing we did was check the fridge." When he was in college, he started to notice certain patterns about the women he dated and what was inside their refrigerator. "Nothing says more about who we are than what we eat or drink. When I look inside someone's fridge, I can get into their head-their lifestyle, their finance. [Take] women who eat meat, I find them more successful." Okaaaay, I think skeptically. But he continues.

"When I got into my thirties and advertising and brands and lifestyles; [I saw] every brand . . . has a target demo. Here is this product. You can see the demographic. Nothing is black and white, but there are universal truths. You can see if [a woman is] healthy, if they take care of themselves, if they drink and entertain."

When he saw his wife's fridge, it dawned on him that this woman was never going to cook for him. "Looking in the fridge on the second date—she didn't have the nurturing 'let me take care of you foods.'" But on the other hand, he says, "She's fun."

I am beginning to buy into his concept. We move on to his Dating Zones. The Dating Zones are those ages in a woman's life when they are looking for different things in a relationship. I share these with you because, although I find them offensive in an overall chauvinistic way and they chafe my feminist core, there is a modicum of truth in them:

> Zone 1. 20-30 years: The First Danger Zone. Every time [these women] go on a date, they are 5 steps ahead, planning. And no matter what a dickbag this guy may be, and he's not that into her, they start getting "wacky-pack," not living in the moment, not flexible. They put so much pressure on themselves to make things work.
>
> Zone 2. 31-35 years: [These] women think: screw this, guys are dicks anyway. "I am ok." They start moving past the danger zone. "I am awesome, my career is going great, I am traveling the world." They start dating and having great experiences. They start realizing that their friends are having kids.
>
> Zone 3. 36-37 years: The Next Danger Zone. Their eggs are drying up. Suddenly there is the pressure all over again. More "wacky-pack."

"So much of this is the women's fault," he says. "NY/LA. I call it the Revenge of the Nerds. 'Nebbishy' little guys who went to Harvard Business School and can get any girl they want now. Women become a [focus of] revenge . . . so many of these women are looking for the 'BBD,' Bigger and Better Deal . . . often women are going after the guy who won't give them what they need."

I fill Stonehill in about Princeton Mom. I am eager to hear what he has to say. "I agree [with her,]" he says in that dudely way of his. "It's much easier to make a nerd cool, then to make a dick nice. A dick is a dick for life." I am so struck by that comment.

I try to pin him down about what traits men are looking for in women they date. It is not easy. He has some strong opinions, like "Ivy League women think they are way hotter than they are." But I want to have some guidelines to bounce off the normal working guys I plan to interview. I want to see if the same traits emerge across the board.

"First, you gotta be healthy. If you are not healthy, I don't want to date you." *I'm warming up a little.* "It will interfere with our life together if you can't do the things I want to do together. Confidence. If you are not confident . . . " he trails off. "It is important that they are comfortable with who they are. Let the guy be the guy." Again, *dudeness.* "Lower expectations. That doesn't mean marry some schlub you are not attracted to, but sex fades. You are looking for a partner for the rest of your life. [You need to] change your expectations for what will make a great husband in life, not someone who is a great partner in your twenties. AND," he holds my attention with a hand in the air. "Stop being the boss. Stop busting balls. Stop going after the unattainable guy." He brings his hand down on the table with conviction. Like a dude. I deduce from this rant that he believes it is okay for men to try and date a woman "out of their league" but women should know their rank and place.

This aspect of the conversation calls to mind Maureen Dowd's book *Are Men Necessary?*:

> So was the feminist movement a cruel hoax? Do women get less desirable as they get more successful? Women want to be in relationship with guys they can seriously talk to—unfortunately, a lot of those guys want to be in relationships with women they don't have to talk to.[2]

What would she say about ChecktheirFridge.com?

Is weight an issue, I ask Stonehill, because one of my experts says it most definitely is.

"I want them to have curves," Stonehill says. "A tush and boobs . . . you are too heavy if you can't accept your own body. If a woman is overweight to the point that she is not comfortable with herself naked, then it's a problem. And I want to see pubic hair. I don't want to date the Kate Moss type. Who wants to shag a woman who looks like a 12-year-old boy?"

Stonehill is also with Landsman on a few other points. "It would never work for me for the women to choose me. The guy has to somehow pursue the girl." It was "100% when I saw my wife. Something was there." And he believes that women still have to make themselves attractive if they are looking for a mate.

But in support of his own sense of branding, he says,

"People tell you if you want to see what a girl will look like in 20 years check out their moms. I say: check their fridge and see if they are eating healthy. I want to see clear evidence that she is making an effort . . . I want to see some guilty pleasures. When I look in their fridge, I want to see someone who is putting their best foot forward. Because if they are not doing it now, they won't later."

The conversation with Stonehill is a bit raw, but I take what I have learned and move on to some men who are currently dating. They are predominantly in their thirties. The first question I ask is what are the traits that they look for in women they want to date. It goes like this:

> Smart, attractive, entertaining
> Attractive, smart, driven, creative
> Attractive, intelligent, not boring
> Confident, intelligent, self-aware, attractive
> Attractive, well-rounded, charming
> Looks, big personality, athletic
> Pretty, intelligent, acceptable to parents

Of these seven men, five list physical appearance as the first trait. Steve elaborates for me: "I am big into looks, but I would rather they have a big personality," he says. "I am looking for someone who is able to hang out and just watch TV. I don't want to have to go out and show off a woman. Don't want someone who wears a lot of makeup. But I do want her to have a career or aspirations to have a career. And I want someone who wants to start a family."

Michael says that in addition to pretty, "she has to be able to carry on a conversation. And she has to be someone I would be proud to bring home to my parents. If they didn't approve, it would fizzle out. Their opinion matters."

"Without the physical attraction, it's very difficult to be stimulated mentally," explains Jordan. "She's got to be sexy, beautiful. It's not a prerequisite that she be a supermodel. But your eye tells you that you want to talk to that woman . . . nature has a weird way of making us want something with the physical eye and that's kind of the beginning of the allure of a woman." He also would like "a well-rounded girl . . . someone who is in balance and is adaptable to take on the world." She should also have "a willingness to be caring and loving to others . . . and charm is a big thing. I tend to gravitate toward a woman who can walk into a room and light it up. That to me is very attractive—a woman who separates herself and has this glowing aura."

"I value two things," says Los Angeles writer Afshin Hatami. "Physical attraction, because I am shallow, and intelligence because there's nothing worse than being bored."

Need I go on? Landsman's contention that physical attraction comes first is proven out in almost every conversation I have with men. And those men who don't say "looks" first, usually lead with "intelligence," but quickly go to looks as their second requirement. Where is humor? Compassion? Likes football? Not very high on the list for most of the men I spoke with.

I continue my conversation Hatami, who writes an online dating advice column and has a hankering for badass women. He provides me with his top ten criteria. I am thrilled to see where "appearance" surfaces on his list.

1. Brains (When our looks fade, we'd both better be attracted to our respective brains)
2. Wit (Keep me on my toes.)
3. Looks (Let's make some good-looking babies)
4. Confidence (Know you're a badass. Own it.)
5. Sense of Humor (If we can't be silly and laugh sometimes/most of the time, then we're both trying too hard.)
6. Style (A girl with a badass sense of style is a huge turn on.)
7. Willingness to spend a Friday night in, drinking wine, eating cheese, listening to good music and dancing like idiots (Because, duh.)
8. Spontaneity (Routine makes things stale real fast.)
9. Ambition (Be awesome. But always keep on wanting to be "awesomer.")
10. Friends (If they are terrible . . . well, that's not a promising sign.)

Hatami's brand is definitely in line with the kind of man I might recommend for the single women I know. He's really good on paper. I take advantage of his good nature and ask him a lot of questions and am pleased that none of the responses involve items that might be in someone's produce drawer. I share his answers with you here in his own words, because, well, they are both helpful and entertaining.

Proper etiquette

As far as etiquette is concerned, I believe the guy should pay, no questions asked, at least during the courtship. Though after the first few dates, it is nice when the girl offers to split the check.

On Manners

Don't be a dick. Open doors, don't bitch about her taking too long to get ready, compliment her. Just simple, decent human being things. Though there is one chivalrous act that is outdated: ordering for your date. You don't know what she wants. Let her make the decision. Sure, offer suggestions, but this isn't the 1930s, she can make up her own mind.

Do men like women who pursue them?

That depends on the amount of games both parties want to play. Of course, it's nice when a girl makes it clear she's interested in you. But at the same time, a little bit of mystery is intriguing. Being too available initially is definitely not attractive.

What advice would you give to women about finding/attracting a man?

I think for both men and women, the best advice I could give is to be happy with yourself first. You'll never find a healthy relationship with someone else, if you don't already have a healthy relationship with yourself.

Should a woman make the first move?

The kind of man that is going to be threatened by a girl that makes the first move, isn't the kind of man you want to attract. It shows some confidence when a girl makes the first move. The guy who is turned off by a girl that makes the first move is living in some archaic, chauvinistic world. Stay away.

Is weight an issue?

I'll be completely honest: weight is an issue. Physical attraction is important. I put a decent amount of effort into my physical appearance, and I appreciate a girl that makes the same kind of effort. But it's funny how quickly physical attraction can change once you get to know the girl. A hot girl with a terrible personality can get quickly get unattractive.

Big job an issue?

I don't think a big job is make or break. Above all, dating a girl that has her shit together, one way or another, is important. That

> doesn't mean she has to be making tons of money. Just that she knows what she wants to do. A girl that's absolutely passionate about what she wants to do is a big turn on. No matter what that is, except accounting. I don't think I could ever date an accountant, that'd be beyond boring. Unless she was secretly a badass chick, who just masqueraded as an accountant.
>
> **Attire as a turn off/turn on?**
> Regardless of personal style, I think it's all about what the girl feels comfortable in. Don't put on an outfit just to "pick up guys". Wear something you feel confident in. Confidence exudes sexy.

Just to be fair, I also ask the men what the biggest turnoffs are, thinking maybe, *just maybe*, there is something to learn here.

Ben from Chicago, is very succinct. "Mean, selfish, racist, fake, bossy, dumb, boring: the normal stuff." *(Normal? He's definitely been meeting the wrong women.)*

Alex: "Obnoxious. Lives in Murray Hill."

David: "Insecure."

Zack: "Needy."

Jordan: "If they are not educated and can't jive with some of the things I am talking about, if they have no clue about obvious world events. Don't just want her on her phone and glued to social media all day long."

Steve: "Not being able to make decisions. You want me to make the decision? I will make it, but you can't complain when I make it. Also smoking. That's a big, big turnoff. And really big girls do not turn me on, but being in shape does."

There is that weight issue again. As someone who grew up chubby and occasionally crossed over into full-out fat, it hurts.

"It's okay," my mother would tell me, after every school social that sent me home in tears. "You have a pretty face." Nah. I am seeing it more clearly now. That just doesn't cut it. "Not fair! Not fair!" screams the fifth-grader cruelly nick-named "Tank" that lives inside me. My heart goes out to the overweight girls.

There are a few more generalizations I can make. I am happy to report that almost every man I spoke with said his parents emphasized that family is the most important thing. Family first. Then career. And that was true even for the men who came from divorced homes. They were also told their primary job in the family is to be the provider. And they want deeply to be good providers, but are not adverse to having wives who make more money than they do. Except Jordan.

Jordan, who is 35, is very clear that although his wife could make more money, he wouldn't want an "alpha female. If she is assertive and also has tact and knows how to use it where it's appropriate, that's okay. But if . . . she becomes a control freak or is dominating, that's a big turnoff. I don't think that would work out too well in the long run for me. Eventually there would be too much of a push and pull in the household for power . . . and not that I am egotistical, machismo or a chauvinist, but I do believe that certain things go back to the traditional values, that men should be providing certain things in the household and women should be providing other things. I understand that that has changed, but if I am going to find myself doing laundry with my future wife, and [later] she could be hammering in nails, I don't want her telling me she is going to be putting an addition on the house."

Yes, the dude *still* wants to be the dude. "Could it be that alpha men do not want to share their alpha zone with alpha women?" asks Dowd.[3]

So, Jordan, I say, tell me where you think women are missing the boat?

"We all have a lot of preconceived notions of who we want to marry. The perfect person. Through social media I think that we are looking for that. People have extremely high and rigid standards and the minute they meet someone and things don't go exactly the way they want, they are going to move on. I hear very beautiful women say 'I am not going to settle.' What aren't you going to settle for? The thing you are obsessing over—the deal breaker—is [usually] not such a big deal . . . expectations have a lot to do with it. Women want perfect. The men, too. Everyone wants the airbrushed image they see in the magazines . . . too high expectations." Is he talking about the BBD? The Bigger and Better Deal?

Jordan is a good example of the tough position some men find themselves in, caught between wanting to be progressive yet steeped in traditional roles. According to Kimmel's *Guyland*:

> Since the traditional traits of femininity—kindness, patience, and nurturance—are antithetical to the definition of 'success' in the public sphere—competency, assertiveness, ambition—women are constantly navigating between the two poles. When they are seen as competent and assertive, they're not seen as feminine; when they are seen as feminine, kind, and caring, they are not seen as competent.[4]

It creates confusion and fear. Dowd says with a wink, "Some guys I know have been fretting for years that they may be rendered obsolete if women get biological and financial independence, learning how to reproduce and refinance without them."[5] Can you imagine what would happen if women learned the mechanics of car maintenance?

And last, but hardly least: what about kids? YES! Yes, and yes. Some are more emphatic than others. Most see themselves coming home, taking off their tie and heading to the ball field to coach both their sons and daughters. These are smart men. They work hard. They want families, but they want to make sure they can provide for those children in an ample way. Which means putting off marriage for now. They are not sure when enough will be enough. They think they will know when the time comes. I tell them, don't wait too long. The eggs won't keep.

When you are ready, I say with a motherly pat on the arm, give me a call. I know some really nice women.

TWELVE

First Comes Love, Then Comes Marriage?

A little history. Bear with me.

"The American family began life in the raggedness of the Colonial era as a kind of organizational Swiss Army knife—many institutions in one convenient place," says *New York Times* reporter Natalie Angier in her comprehensive article, "The Changing American Family" November 25, 2013. She goes on to say that the home was a place of business where all able-bodied members from toddlers and up contributed in all facets of life. "[It] was a delivery ward, schoolroom, hospital and funeral parlor. Everyone had to reside in the all-encompassing embrace of a bustling household and adults who tried to live alone . . . were viewed with suspicion."

Angier continues with America's curious nature, which "encouraged a degree of footlooseness, a scorn for the settled and a yen for the new." This adventurous spirit "applied as much to conjugal matters as economic ones, and the divorce rate rose steadily along with the number of stars on the flag."

Women rejected the "bustling household" as their only means of gratification and went in search of new opportunities, as they should. They had labor saving devices like washing machines and dishwashers and paper plates.

"When women's life choices were highly constrained, they had little negotiating power," writes Pepper Schwartz in the

CNN Online article "Why More Women Choose Not To Marry.":

> They had to marry or were seen as damaged. A few got away with being "free spirits" but usually they were exceptional in wealth or lineage—and even so, it wasn't easy.
>
> It's different now. While most women still want marriage, they don't want it at just any price. They don't want it if it scuttles their dreams. Marriage is not dead—not by a long shot. It is still, to most of us, the house we wish to build for our love, our lover and our children.
>
> But women want to craft a life instead of having it pressed upon them. And that means some of us will be single for a long time, and some of us will be single for life.[1]

On the path to crafting that life, women delay childbearing, sometimes missing the fertility window completely. As a whole, they have less children but more interesting jobs. And more fun, some might claim. But not all of them. The women of this book are single and childless, yes, but not by choice. I think about *this* sad reality, as I sip my cup of steaming ginger tea and worry about the next generation.

I personally feel the conundrum. What does it mean for our children? And in a world where there are more women than men, what does it mean for our daughters? Just in Manhattan alone, the women outnumber the men by tens of thousands. This report is from 2006, and standing in line at a Midtown Starbucks on any given afternoon will back it up. The data is based on trends predicted from 2000 census data.[2]

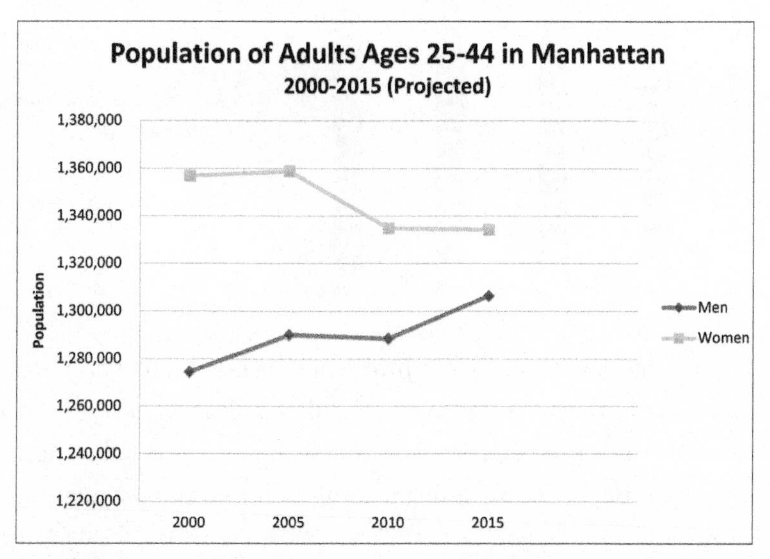

	Male	Female	Difference
2000	1,274,434	1,356,867	82,433
2005	1,289,977	1,358,834	68,857
2010	1,288,402	1,334,907	46,505
2015	1,306,294	1,334,374	28,080

The research tells us there are not enough men for all the women and that marriage is not only happening later, it is on the decline. Less marriage = less babies. OY! What's a Jewish (wanna-be grand-)mother to do? Ask a priest. *Ask a priest??* Yes.

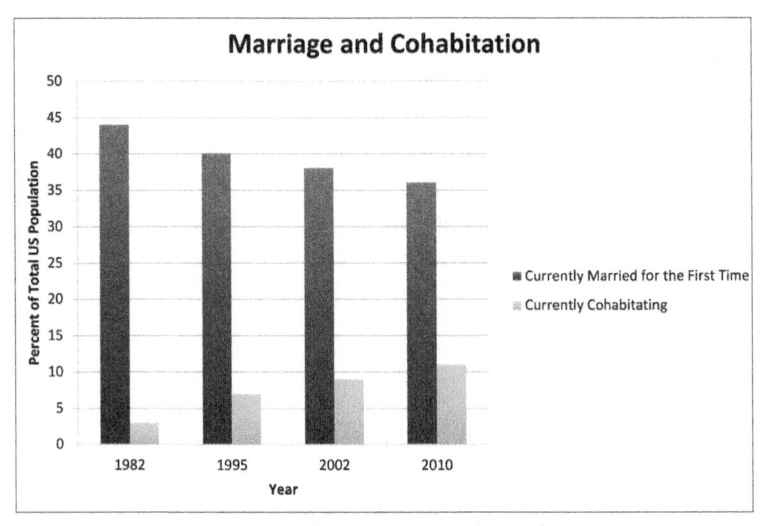

Tell me it isn't so, Father Jim! Not that I have any reason to endorse marriage, based on my childhood. But I am trying to look forward, not back. And although the rate of cohabitation is on the rise, it doesn't indicate an upswing in the production of babies.

Rev. James DiLuzio C.S.P. (Community of Saint Paul) is a friend from grade school with whom I have reconnected in my adult life. One of the reasons Father Jim is so dear to me—aside from his wisdom, gentle nature and ability to critique a work of writing without hurting my feelings!—is rooted in our middle school years. This was a terrible time for my family, with frequent calls to the police because of domestic violence. That's what they call it these days in the NFL and other places. That's politically correct, right? But I would rather be frank with you. It's more graphic, but more accurate: the police came to our house when my father was beating the shit out of my mother.

Father Jim's dad was Officer DiLuzio. In my world, he was the soft-voiced, soft-hearted policeman who took us out of the room and calmed us while the other cops read my father the riot act or sent him out of the house to cool down. How many other homes did they enter every week to perform the same task? I don't know. But I do know that when the call for assistance went out over the police radio, every Tom, Dick and Harry in our town who had access to that police radio knew that there was a "situation" in the big split level on the East Hill with the wood-sided station wagon out front. And almost every house that heard that call had at least one kid who went to school with my brothers and me. And at least one of those kids felt it necessary to make a big deal about it at school the next day. But it was never Jim. I never got a "heard your dad was beating up on your mom again" from him. Never even a curious look. Was it his father's discretion or his? I don't know, but I appreciated it, nevertheless. So when we reconnected at a high school reunion, I let him know how much that meant.

In the ensuing years, our relationship has brought me much comfort and satisfaction, so it was natural to turn to him for some higher insight about the state of marriage. At least in the Roman Catholic Archdiocese of New York. I knew it wouldn't be the whole picture, but it follows the trend for the secular world. And since it's *my* research, I have to admit it's really fun to snuggle into one of the overstuffed wing chairs in the dark, wood-paneled rectory library at Church of Saint Paul the Apostle in Manhattan and have a philosophical conversation with a man of religion.

Father Jim still has the boyish handsomeness that must have helped during his years as an actor in musical theater and his voice still resonates rhythmically, as though he might sing at any moment. He has been thinking a lot about my topic in preparation for our meeting and he opens with a strong overture.

"In terms of the church's understanding of marriage, it's a culmination of deep friendship that comes to be expressed both physically, emotionally, intellectually—a sense of faith—and a sense of experiencing God in one's love making, in one's collaboration and in one's ongoing forgiveness whether for the petty little things in life or human foibles and idiosyncrasies in our body habits," he says. That's a tall order, I tell him, and far removed from the economic necessities Angier lays out in her NY Times piece.

"Its such an ideal, its an all encompassing continual self-giving, mutual-supporting ideal. I think for many today, it's too much, because society compartmentalizes aspects of the human person a great deal, to its detriment. You have the intellectual self, with all its rigor. You have the sexual self . . . I think there has been a real divorce between sexuality and spirituality. Unfortunately, to a large degree, culturally, it's like an entitlement vs. a relationship."

He tells me about a couple he counseled who had great disagreement in their marriage and one day, during a session, one of them blurted out, "This is hard work."

"Yes it is." Father Jim replied. "It really *is* hard work to be attentive to another one's feelings, to be in touch with yours. When you are angry, it's a secondary emotion. You have to see what's underneath. It's usually some kind of fear or deep hurt, and those are harder to reveal. And sometimes we don't even know what we are feeling right away." And there is always the option to just walk away and never explore those feelings. Kind of like my father, who refused to even talk to a therapist or our rabbi. *He* didn't have a problem. It wasn't until many years later, in my forties that I started to explore what my parents' deep fears and hurts were. It was the beginning of forgiving them.

I know marriage is hard, I sigh, but what is stopping this generation from getting there in the first place? They are falling in love. They are moving in together. But they are not making that lasting, formal commitment.

"I think that the young couples today are very absorbed in their work and their careers, but they still want company. [They have] a basic human loneliness and longing for another but they don't have the time to put into the relational dynamic."

Father Jim explains to me that the protocol for a marriage physically within a Catholic church requires three appointments with a priest before the marriage sacrament is given. "[We] look at what they have commonly acknowledged or already worked through in their relationship: aspects of what it means to be a friend, a lover, what it means to collaborate about finances . . . and I believe for some, if they are not regular church goers, it's just too much. For the more upwardly mobile young couples, they are too busy. Their jobs call for them to travel a lot."

I notice that friendship comes up often in his discussion of marriage, both within the marriage and outside of it and I ask him—off topic—if he has any feelings about the recent trend to have friends as officiants at modern ceremonies. His hearty laugh cuts through the quiet reverence of the library.

"I think it's a riot!" he exclaims, "but there is an ambiguity. They want something spiritual . . . even when they have their friends officiate . . . they want someone who knows them. All of that *is* spiritual. It's just not formally spiritual. What is different is this autonomy. They think they have to reinvent the wheel."

He is ruminating on this topic and the room gets quiet again. I can hear the many conversations of the past echo off the walls covered in portraits of past priests. These long-gone men of God are listening to *our* conversation, their quiet demeanors unruffled with deliberation. I look at their faces, their painted eyes and wonder what religious and social quandaries have graced this space and what they would make of today's world.

"Maybe it is all too individual-centered," Father Jim says, cutting through my reverie, bringing me back to the present. "They start from scratch because it has to be all about 'us.' But marriage is reminding you that it isn't all about you, its part of a bigger story—its about community, its about how you as a couple will fit into society."

Kate Bolick of the *Atlantic* expressed these concerns in an article she wrote in 2011, referencing an old boyfriend:

> The decision to end a stable relationship for abstract rather than concrete reasons ("something was missing"), I see now, is in keeping with a post-Boomer ideology that values emotional fulfillment above all else. And the elevation of independence over coupling ("I wasn't ready to settle down") is a second-wave feminist idea I'd acquired from my mother, who had embraced it, in part, I suspect, to correct for her own choices.

We speak at length about this generation, their self-absorption and their trauma, which may very well be linked. They are the children of divorce. And although I am not *of* this generation, I relate deeply and personally. Father Jim believes that we have not yet fully explored the damage of these splintered families in terms of "the hurts and the wounds, the subliminal stuff. We still haven't helped one another's families communicate well, how to deal with uncomfortable situations, how to express anger."

Having started out as a teacher, he still thinks in terms of education. "I have often thought there has to be a course on how to be a family, as well as lovers and friends, from kindergarten right through high school. It's as important as math and science and English. It's what is at the heart of life. We would be giving society a tremendous gift." Still, he cautions, "You would be on a fine line in America with personal liberty [as] this is intrusive in the family. The truth is, though, if your family is really unhealthy, like in marriage, it's not just about you, or your family. This hurt overflows into the workplace and into the school and everything else."

We talk about many things and I ask him if there are any cold, hard facts about the decline in marriage and he offers to contact the office of the Archdiocese of New York. Sister Eileen Clifford generously sends me a substantial pile of numbers for New York City. I have combined all categories of Catholic marriage here: Catholic to Catholic, Catholic to Other Christian, Catholic to Non-Christian into one number to illustrate the overall decline in church marriages.

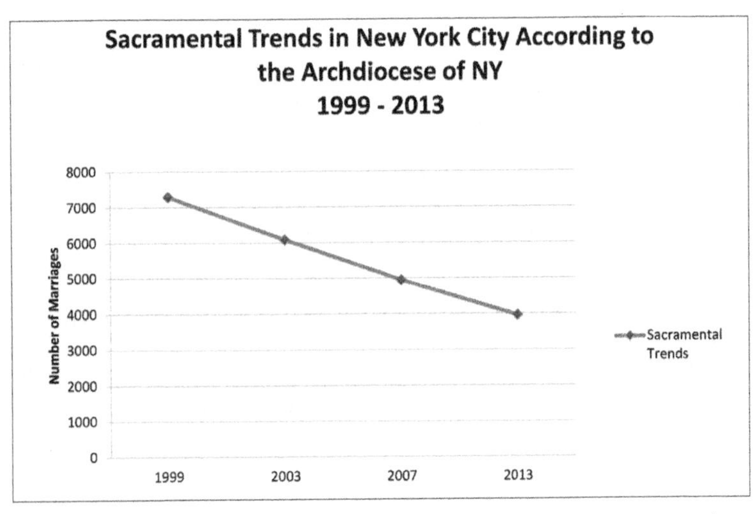

Its such a dramatic nosedive, its frightening. "We used to have a wedding almost every weekend in our church," says Father Jim, of his beautiful sanctuary on the Upper West Side. "Mostly now they fall during the big wedding seasons in the spring and fall."

Is interfaith marriage a component, I ask, and the priest surfaces. "That's what the Bible is really about," he says. "The story of God calling people out of a tribal way of living into a universal brotherhood. Tribal brings a sense of identity and cohesion. Every group starts that way. We can't help it, it's genetic. [But] I don't think young people are thinking that way—the conflict between the tribal and the universal. Seeing religion as part of the tribal is one of the reasons young people don't want to get involved with traditional marriage."

He is also looking at the changing nature of couples. "I call it the *Fiddler On The Roof* syndrome. That play, the whole highlight of the second act is acceptance of what you don't expect for your children. One by one, they married someone who didn't fit the expectation." One son-in-law didn't have a good monetary future; another had different political views. "The last one was a Christian and was outside of the group. It's a universal and it's very important to come to some sort of acceptance. It's almost subversive for us not to talk about acceptance, because there is a deep human drive to preserve traditions. [We are] afraid of things getting lost." And that's if they marry at all.

"The typical American Family, if it ever lived anywhere but on Norman Rockwell's Thanksgiving canvas, has become as multilayered and full of surprise as a holiday turducken," writes Angier.[3] She then comments on researchers who have studied the evolution of the American family structure and how rapidly it has been changing in recent years. "Blacks marry whites, atheists marry Baptists, men marry men and women, women, Democrats marry Republicans and start talk shows. Good friends join forces as part of the 'voluntary kin' movement, sharing medical directives, wills, even adopting one another legally."

For many of the mothers I have spoken with while researching this book, there is a tradeoff. They shrug and say, sure, we would love to have a church (or temple) wedding, but she's in her late thirties. We are just happy she found *someone*! Having their child in a relationship with a person they love who loves them back, in the end, seems to trump tradition.

I am reluctant to bring up hookup culture, but *really*, who better to discuss sex with than a priest? And his sensibility is so heartfelt that it appeals to my deepest sentimental ideal of romantic love. So, what *does* he think of hooking up?

"You can get the sexual fulfillment and affection," says

Father Jim, who came to the priesthood in his thirties. "I think that's been part of the separation of sexuality from its other components. The reason faith discourages casual sex and/or sex without a lifetime commitment is all the possibilities for deep wounds. Because one's sense of worth and self esteem is tied to one's body . . . when you are sharing your body and that other person doesn't give you full acceptance or any kind of commitment it can create a sense of worthlessness and deep hurt."

In support of that, Kathleen Bogel writes in *Hooking Up: Sex, Dating, and Relationships on Campus*, that in spite of sexual freedom, women still have to be concerned with their reputation. "Even though most males still engage multiple hook-up partners each semester, a female who does the same is labeled a 'slut.'"[4] The potential for lasting hurt is inherent. She goes on to say that "Females are more likely to go further sexually with someone they are not interested in pursuing a relationship with,"[5] which is a kind of crazy reversal of the whole culture, and yet in direct support of Father Jim's contention that sex and spirituality have parted ways.

In *The End of Sex: How Hookup Culture is Leaving a Generation Unhappy, Sexually Unfulfilled, and Confused About Intimacy*, author Donna Freitas says:

> The great irony of hookup culture—whether pre-, during, or post-college—is that it's ultimately a culture of repression. If the Victorian era represents the repression of sexual desire, then the era of hookup is about the repression of romantic feeling, love, and sexual desire, too, in favor of greater access to sex—sex for the sake of sex.[6]

> *Everyone* has something to say about sex. If you doubt me, just get back in line at that Starbucks. You can hear a whole dissertation on who's having it, not getting any, wanting it, or is giving it up forever. And that's just while waiting for your caramel macchiato.

Kate Bolick writes in the November 2011 issue of the *Atlantic Monthly* that "according to Robert H. Frank, an economist at Cornell who has written on supply and demand in the marriage market . . . when the available women significantly outnumber men . . . social norms against casual sex will weaken."

"It's far more complex," suggests Father Jim. "Sometimes [within] society, and even medicine and science, there is a tendency to look at the body as a machine instead of a soul-infused person. So again, it's your check list: I am taking care of my mind, I am taking care of my genitals, I am taking care of my heart and my breathing . . . we are still on that quest for what is the whole person."

And modern women have embraced this desire for wholeness. With the emergence of the Women's Movement, the directive—and often the financial need—for women to go out and achieve has changed the face of the family. When women no longer need the protection of a husband or marriage, they can perpetuate the species with the help of some purchased sperm and a good nanny. So what happens to the men?

"The subliminal collective unconscious of the male has become almost defiant because an old traditional foundation has been taken away. Men have to redefine their roles. The old definitions no longer work," says Father Jim. "There are advantages and disadvantages. The benefit is it requires more self-evaluation . . . the whole Peter Pan syndrome: eternal adolescent men. I am tired of them; I don't find them funny. That's one of the backlashes: 'let's just have the toys.'

In some ways, feminism co-opted that. 'This is my empowerment . . . I'll have sex with whomever I want.' A sense of intimacy and partnership comes off the table . . . and because of the self-scrutiny, men realize how essential the partnership really is . . . and sharing vulnerability—how beautiful and empowering a life-giving force it is."

That's a nice image—of the man in touch with his emotional, feminine side—but Bolick paints a different picture:

> If, in all sectors of society, women are on the ascent, and if gender parity is actually within reach, this means a marriage regime based on men's overwhelming economic dominance may be passing into extinction . . . now that we can pursue our own status and security, and are therefore liberated from needing men the way we once did, we are free to like them more, or at least more idiosyncratically, which is how love ought to be, Isn't it?[7]

Yes. Yes, I believe it is.

But is that what we have taught our daughters? I am afraid to think that maybe we have omitted that piece. Maybe what we conveyed about financial independence has overshadowed the message that it is just plain nice to have a partner. To share the journey, and reflect together on the joys and challenges of living. To put your cold feet against someone's warm hairy legs on a chilly winter night. To sit together at the end of the day, and feel secure in each other's presence. No competition. No dominance. Just a peaceful, cooperative coexistence.

We wind up our conversation with a simple scientific reality that for some people will obliterate the whole previous discussion of sex, marriage, economy and spirituality: we are simply living longer. We live and act sequentially; there is always time for that next "thing," whether it is a trip, an advanced degree, a new career, a baby . . . or even marriage. It's another thing to put on the back burner while we are having a good time living our lives. Only problem is, when it comes to getting pregnant, you can't. The clock is still ticking.

A SENSE OF SHAME

Elizabeth is a 43-year-old attractive blonde woman with a quick wit, a sharp analytical mind and an infectious laugh, who looks 15 years younger than her chronological age. I have known her for over 10 years and watched her change from an optimistic young artist and career woman with plans for a family to a resolute middle aged woman bordering on bitter and then back to the sunny disposition I first encountered. She has had quite a trip and is still traveling, so to speak.

Born in Germany, she spent her first seven years in Berlin. The next seven were spent in a very rural part of the Catskills, two hours north of New York City. Her parents then returned to Berlin. She was home-schooled until high school, when she finally entered a mainstream environment. "I didn't date in high school." She shrugs her shoulders. "I think I was I was very undeveloped in that area." Although her mother was wonderful and supportive, she had no dating information to give

Elizabeth, no strategies to help her through the mating ritual.

"My parents met on the way to college orientation. Dad was 17 and Mom was 18. They were together from that moment on. My mother had never dated anyone else. In their mythology, you meet someone and you are with them for the rest of your lives."

"The template of that relationship is from an earlier time and wasn't really going to work for me." Elizabeth says she has spent a good part of her life "always waiting to 'just meet someone.' I didn't understand you should date someone just for the experience of it."

With parents who truly love each other and are good friends, and a mother who was an exemplary role model for her time, a teacher until she had children, Elizabeth had high expectations of a relationship. She really didn't begin dating in earnest until she was 24 and out of graduate school. "If I met someone and it wasn't kismet, I moved on," she says.

Although Internet dating was just becoming an option, it didn't "fit the narrative" she had grown up with, so Elizabeth didn't explore online opportunities until she was in her early thirties. "I should have started that in my mid to late twenties and I didn't." But she soon found herself in a significant relationship that lasted several years.

Despite her parents' successful union, Elizabeth thinks the chances of having a relationship that goes the distance are pretty slim. She credits television with part of her poor image of marriage. "The sitcoms were mostly written by men who hate their wives," she learned in a writing class in Los Angeles. "I think that has changed now. The [writers] came out of being comedians, who are not the happiest people to begin with, and divorce was so new and prevalent."

She says the strongest argument she has seen in favor of marriage is on a practical level. With her parents nearing 80 now, "there is a huge benefit to having someone else there to take care of you . . . I think you are fine until about 65 or 70, but then you become very vulnerable without someone there looking out for you . . . I have women friends going into their sixties who made a choice when they were in their forties that they were fine being single, now they wish they had someone around, even like a buddy."

Elizabeth has strong views on the roles society has imposed on the sexes. "I am definitely a feminist, by that I mean men and women are equal. But the one thing that is finally bubbling to the surface in our culture is this: we have this idea that what men value and think is the norm, and what we have is derivative or a different idea. It's finally reaching the point where women are starting to say that we are just *different*."

"This has been a brilliant system for men for the last thousand years," she says, laying out the argument at the heart of the women's movement. "There are two groups of people and one group gets to leave the house and do a lot of work. Men go out and do stuff. There is a difference based on strength, and some things are more interesting than other things. Caring for children is stimulating on some level, but the rest of it—the things nobody wants to do—is what women do." She points out that now, due to the economics of raising a family, "so many women go to work all day and come home and have two jobs." She says recent statistics have men doing only 25% of the housework even if they both work.

Elizabeth can spin the numbers and quote the rhetoric

of the Women's Movement like a college professor. She reads about it, she writes about it, she understands how difficult it is. She *lives* it. But she is most compelling when she speaks about the emotional cost of not marrying.

"I think the biggest imperative to marry, the reason we still want it even in today's climate, is there is still a huge shame factor to not having found a husband. Moving forward by yourself? When push comes to shove, everyone is a little embarrassed by it . . . there is this sense of 'if you really wanted this, you would have settled down and picked someone and not been such a princess.' Those people who love you will be fine with it, but after the 1950s, we got the idea in this culture that there was a certain progression that had to happen: finding the right guy, marrying, having a kid with a man you love. You would be this family."

Elizabeth discusses how her mainstream Christian upbringing impacts her outlook. "I don't know how different it is in any other group, but there is a real sense that if God—however you define God—wanted this to happen in your life, it would have happened. You are going against nature trying to do this without a man . . . and this brings up a lot of strong emotions from people. I remember from my teen years reading endless articles, fear-mongering, that if you were single over 35 you had a better chance being hit by a cab, creating fear that you have to pick someone. Which goes back to shame. **There is something in our culture about someone marrying you that validates you as a woman.** *(I have put this is bold because I think it is an essential truth in this discussion.)* It proves you have value. When no one marries you or validates you, you are strangely invisible to other people, at family events, also at work. Woman who have married and have kids have a higher status."

Elizabeth touches a nerve for me. Am I guilty of this? Is the whole act of writing this book a validation of her hypothesis: there is something "other" about women who have not married and had children? But they *want* to, I think defensively. Even Elizabeth, for all her political fury, *wants* to be married. But she is correct; we somehow assign blame—or confer pity—on those who aren't. *(The shame is on us.)*

"I am in my forties," Elizabeth continues, "and at family events, they can put you at the children's table. On vacation, you get the fold-out couch." An arrow pierces my heart —I am guilty of this! *(Forgive me, dear daughter.)* "You literally do not have the same status as the marrieds."

Elizabeth continues to make her case: "My mother was one of seven and I have forty cousins. They are all married with kids, I am the only one who isn't married."

She finally met someone when she was 38. "We were in a serious relationship, building a future," and then it ended. Don't even ask! She shakes her head. "I was 40, and barring some sort of Hollywood miracle, there was no way, no time left to meet someone, have a normal relationship that would lead to a family. There was a good year-and-a-half grieving period and then I realized if I was going to move forward on my own [to have a child], it's going to be a completely different picture of what I thought I would always have. And that is the hardest part, the hardest thing to let go of. When you do finally let go of it, there is such a relief. You can't feel bad forever."

She admits that there are moments that are more difficult than others. "Sometimes I see a cute family on the street with a dad helping his kids and I get a pang of grief." But she is not done with her dream of a relationship. "Maybe I will meet someone else afterwards. It will be a different picture. I don't want my [future] child to never have a relationship with a father figure. You worry about screwing them up."

As much as Elizabeth wants a baby and is going forward alone, she still thinks in terms of partnership. "I want someone to do stuff with, someone to share the decision-making and financial burden with . . . I want someone to talk about my TV shows with, to share my day. One of the hardest things about being single is that you have no one to bounce things off of, like insurance, the car. It's easier as a couple . . . even with a division of labor, some big stuff you figure out together."

Elizabeth is an incredibly social woman with a full extra-curricular life. It surprises me that she still feels so alone. What about her brothers, girlfriends or guy friends, I ask her. "When you don't have the sexual and romantic connection, when push comes to shove, you are still making decisions by yourself. There is a reason this system exists throughout the animal kingdom. It does make things easier. But the system is crumbling . . . it's been this way for thousands of years and it's gone through a colossal change in only the last fifty years. I think it's going to take hundreds of years before it becomes something else."

She also thinks a lot about the religious implications. "In a weird way, they are right, the conservatives, because in the long term if we uncouple having children from necessarily having to do it with a man we have made a commitment to, the (men) will lose a lot of power. Then the only thing they will bring to the table with us is their personality."

And she doesn't want to lose the men at the table. "I think men have just as much to bring . . . guys always help me in emergencies," she says. "The rescue element—they are mechanical and procedural. They want to do it and they love to do it, and I have learned to let them . . . some days, I just want [a man] to give me a hug. When you are single—other than your mom giving you a hug—no one else touches you, ever. We want someone to touch us, to pet us. I think it's a basic need. We want intimacy, we want someone to hug us after a bad day, to hold hands." And she is not talking about a manicure or massage at the corner shop.

But there is also this: "For single women, in their late thirties to forties, who have had a certain amount of autonomy and power, it's hard to integrate someone into your life . . . if you've been single for 20 years, you aren't used to thinking about someone else." She has obviously considered every angle of this dilemma and specifically articulates the argument that Father Jim has raised about a generation that places individual happiness at the forefront

There is a lot of help for those who do decide to go forward alone and I ask Elizabeth if she has explored Single Mothers by Choice. "What bothers me about Single Mothers By Choice is that I feel like I am becoming a single mother by *default*. I wanted to get married and I wanted to have kids. It was the single most important thing in my life. This is Plan B. I don't feel like it was really a *choice* on my part, but I need to make something of my life." Knowing her accomplishments as a gifted artist, I am saddened that she views having a child as the way to "make something of her life." She has *already* made a significant contribution, baby or no baby.

Elizabeth has a renewed sense of hope as she enters into the world of fertility centers. Although she has spent thousands of dollars on IVF, egg freezing and fertility drugs, she feels good about having a plan of action. "There is a real sense of freedom [in] moving forward and I feel happy about myself. I don't want to be 50 and be 'me and my cat.' I want to have a group. We are pack animals. Whatever that group will look like, it won't look like I thought it would, but whatever it is, I *am* going to make that group. I am going to figure it out."

So, this is what I am thinking: yes, we did this. In our earnestness and personal frustration, we have raised daughters who think a man is incidental. Nice to have, but not required. We didn't teach our girls the subtleties of the mating game or impart the balance of female capability and vulnerability. As my next-door neighbor (married, thirties, works full-time and has two-year-old twin girls) said to me when we met over a dog walk along the river on an early spring day, "It's nice to have someone to take out the garbage. You *can* do it alone, its just better to have a partner. But having a partner requires compromise." And is compromise something we introduced into the conversation? I am not sure we did.

I think that in our desire to give our girls the world, we forgot to teach them that it isn't "all or nothing." It doesn't diminish feminine power when a man opens the door, holds your coat, or takes out the recycling. Courtesy and division of labor are not deal breakers. It doesn't undermine your independence if you share the journey. You *can* do it all alone, but that doesn't mean you *have* to.

THIRTEEN

Tea and Demographics

I am looking for help to tell the Jewish story of marriage statistics so that I might have a somewhat more religiously balanced view of the situation. Dr. Ariela Keysar is an accomplished demographer and associate research professor for the public policy and law program at Trinity College in Connecticut. I have come to her through personal connections, She is the sister of my friend Connie's sister-in-law. This is what is called Jewish Geography. I am told that I must speak with Ariela. So I call.

Keysar invites me to meet at her home. It is several miles north of New York City in a pretty bedroom community with a duck pond through the middle of town. The house looks more like a storybook cottage than a suburban dwelling; there is gingerbread trim on the steep, peaked roofline and a touch of red bordering the gables. As I ring the doorbell, I am thinking Hansel & Gretel. Instead, I am greeted by a petite woman who radiates immense energy.

We meet twice. The first time is to walk in the crisp, autumn air and get acquainted. We kick through colored leaves, side-step gullies of acorns. She wants to understand not just what I am writing about, but why. The second time we meet, we almost get right down to business. But first, a little something to nosh.

Her mother has just visited from Israel and has left Keysar with an array of wonderful teas, nuts and dried fruit. "Eat." she says as she offers me little plates of goodies while she prepares a deliciously aromatic brew. "How can we talk without a little something?" Her hospitality is at once relaxing and disarming.

"I am researching dating, mating and grandparenting," I tell her.

"Grandparenting! Ai! It is so important!" The lilt of her Israeli upbringing is evident in her voice and the occasional use of Hebrew words she translates for me as she speaks. She is rapid fire and I listen hard to keep up with her.

Her main area of study is Jewish intermarriage. It seems the Jews are having the same problems as the Catholics. "Ever since 1995, more Jews have married non-Jews than fellow Jews," Keysar says, "and now the rate is at a record high of 58% . . . in fact, fewer of them bother formally to marry: the marriage rate appears to have declined since 2000 (down from 60% in 2000-2001 to 51% today) mirroring a decline in marriage rates among Americans overall. Younger Jews are even more extreme in terms of all these dynamics. Coupled with their low level of fertility (below replacement level), they are moving far away from specifically Jewish attachments and identity."

It seems to me that tradition, religious traditions specifically, are out of fashion. And this is why Keysar gets so excited about grandparenting. She believes that it is the grandparents who can be the preservers of culture. She is looking at the larger picture.

We speak about the rising age of women giving birth for the first time and alternative families. "For young people, with fertility extended, they think: I will figure it out," she says.

"Parents who want to be grandparents have to adjust. They adjust to women having babies out of wedlock, because they want the baby. They pay for the fertility treatment. They have the time, money, and they see the need for the next generation. Continuity. They want to see their name continue . . . grandparents look ahead. If you want continuity, you have to have replacement of the generations."

Much of what she says about marriage is incredibly similar to what Father Jim reported. "Religious marriage is not a mandate anymore," she tells me. "It's a choice. It's a very, very diverse community and you have to make an effort. The constraints are making it harder to carry on your religion, especially when it doesn't seem necessary. You can get married by a Justice of the Peace. Couples want to write their own ceremony. In Israel, they say, 'our gay friends cannot be married by the rabbinate, so we won't be either. We will create our own. We can do it our way, with equality.'" She adds that in some cases, both bride and groom break the glass, a Jewish wedding tradition signifying the remembrance of the destruction of the ancient Temple in Jerusalem, a tempering of joy with the recollection of sorrow. "So much is changing, [I am] not sure that all the churches and synagogues are adjusting to all these changes, and they are left behind."

And again . . . choices. Coming from Israel, Keysar is very conscious of American choices. "How long does it take me in the supermarket?" She laughs and shakes her head. It is a world full of options. "For me as a scientist, I look at the variables in the choices. Your choices have to be compartmentalized, even within that you have choices. Religion gives you choices on your reproductive rights. Do they push for early age marriages?

Are there contraception restrictions? Choices of when to get married? If that's not on your radar because you want to pursue your education and want to be financially independent, you are putting those things at the forefront."

But what about babies, I ask. Keysar responds, "When they settle down and they are 30, you see many girls in the same situation. The women feel empowered . . . they can go to a bar, to the gym, all the cultural activities, because they are not home with a baby. Even travel is now geared for the single women. Women are comfortable going into a restaurant alone, having a meal by themselves. They are independent and economically equal. Now the girls are also competitive; they have the opportunity for freedom of choice. Use contraceptives, pay for it yourself. They're not limited . . . but they don't understand. There is a race and they don't understand that at age 40 you cannot do what you can do at age 26, 27, 28 . . . they have the education, the funds and then they wake up and see they are missing something."

Keysar lays much of the responsibility of delayed childbearing on egalitarian childrearing, a positive result of the Women's Movement, and I find this argument compelling. "The Millennials, those who were born in the 1980s plus, [were] labeled the 'born digital generation.' Not only have they learned about the computer, they were raised with all the gadgets and they cannot live without them. Their frame of mind, their activity is all around the psychology [of being] born into the digital age. What we find, which is fascinating, is that they were exposed to egalitarian education."

When she was doing a study of American Jewish college students, the findings were provocative. "59% of respondents were women and 41% men, reflecting the larger female student presence on U.S. campuses today,"[1] she reported. "Girls have the same commitment, the same obligations as boys." It's a stunning figure and tribute to the parents who made it happen. But let's think 10 years down the road: more women in professions, less women at home. A huge demographic shift. I say it's going to change how families function forever. It is support for Elizabeth's comment that the old system is crumbling.

"Gender is out," Keysar declares. "Take sports: both boys and girls are encouraged to do sports, which is huge. You seriously don't see a difference between the boys and the girls . . . parents are raising their kids the same way, but they don't stay the same, as they mature they take different paths . . . [this] happens before college. Computer technology is mostly boys. It's a field where you don't have boys and girls on par."

Keysar is a living example of the change in women's roles and opportunities. Her mother was born in Yemen where there are no educational opportunities for girls and moved to Israel where she completed eight years of formal education in one year. Now her daughter has a PhD. All that in only one generation.

"I finished my PhD at 35, then started looking for a husband . . . I remember telling my mother 'I don't want a husband like you have.' He was like a sheik. I didn't want to serve my man. My mother was so busy catering to everyone else, she couldn't develop to her potential."

She says most women at that age who want to be married and have a family, do. "[There was a lot] of compromise," she says of her own situation. "It was almost either/or. When you feel you can do the same thing as men, you don't want to take orders or be second choice. But there was a cost." Which brings us back to the fertility experts. Keysar and her husband have a son. But it wasn't easy and they needed their help.

"And now, my son studies with all these girls. Once you knew who you were going to marry: a Jewish boy from your synagogue. It's not happening anymore." Always a scientist looking for cause and effect, Keysar posits: "Here is another speculation, like the kibbutz[2]—you don't marry someone from the kibbutz . . . it's like marrying your brother. They really feel equal. It takes away some of the sexual tension. You don't think of them as mates . . . you want the exotic."

I stir the tea leaves at the bottom of my cup. I wish I could foretell the future by gazing at the soggy remnants pooling there. I think about what Keysar has said. Equality. Freedom of choice. Grandparents as preservers of the culture. What good is preservation if there is no one to pass it on to?

FOURTEEN

Courage To Go It Alone

My daughter tells me that if she isn't partnered with a man she loves by the time she is in her late thirties, she will consider having a child by herself. She has already explored this option with a good friend of hers who has offered his sperm towards the effort. He is smart, extremely talented and very handsome. He is genetically gifted. He himself has no interest in fatherhood beyond that of his scruffy terrier. A gay man engaged to be married, with parenthood nowhere in his plans, he is more than willing to donate to the cause.

They have talked about this, bandied about the possibilities in the way my generation might have discussed carpools. Although a daring proposition to me, it is a real option, one that does not seem foreign to my daughter's generation. Why not, she says.

Why not, indeed. Just ask Single Mothers by Choice. SMC is an international organization comprised of the population it is named for, and those who wish to be. I have been referred to this group by almost every professional I have interviewed. They see it as the natural progression for women without partners who come to them for help with fertility or support for the emotional issues surrounding the quest for a child. With over 50 chapters in the U.S., Canada, Europe, Australia and beyond, they service more than 30,000 members. The average

age of an SMC member is 35. Of those who do successfully conceive a baby, about 60 percent do so by donor insemination and approximately 20 percent adopt. The remaining 20 percent have become pregnant with either a "known donor" or sex partner, although they are raising their child alone.

To fully understand what the organization does and how it came into being, I visit its founder, the kind and generous Jane Mattes, LCSW who carved out a good chunk of time to talk to me. With hands folded in a ladylike manner *(what a crazy old fashioned expression—but apt)* in her lap and feet propped comfortably on an ottoman, I sit catty-corner from her on a cushy couch in her office. My laptop is propped open and ready, as she patiently explores every question I ask, offering her perspective as a therapist as well as a pioneer. She hands me a copy of her book *Single Mothers by Choice* for further research. I tuck the book carefully into my bag, mindful not to bend the pages or scuff the cover, should I need to present it to my daughter at some later date.

Mattes beams with pride as she speaks about the organization she birthed as well as her 34-year-old son, who recently became engaged. "The biological issue is what drives this organization," says Mattes, who created it out of her own need at the age of 36 when she found herself pregnant by a lover who had no interest in being a father. "[The members] struggle with how long to wait, knowing the clock is ticking and the eggs are aging."

She understands them completely. "I was blissfully ignorant how challenging it would be. I had no idea how the alone part would make it so much harder. My mother stopped working and was there for me . . . her devotion made a big difference."

It is more than ironic—I find it karmic—that Mattes' first professional job after receiving her master's degree in social work in 1966 was at a residence for unmarried teenaged girls. They were sent there "to hide their pregnancies (in order to spare themselves and their families the shame of exposure) prior to giving up their babies to married couples for adoption."[1]

"After going through the long and rigorous training required to be a psychoanalyst, I felt sure nothing could be as hard," she writes in her book. "I was wrong—being the mother of a newborn was, for me, much harder. I needed support."[2] She put out the word to everyone she knew that she was looking to connect with women in a similar circumstance. She chose a date and invited them all to her home. Eight women showed up. They bonded quickly and scheduled their next meeting. And then the next.

An article in *The New York Times* followed. This article "proved to be the turning point in our becoming a national organization. [It was] syndicated in newspapers all across the country. Suddenly we were deluged with mail and phone calls requesting information, support, anything we could offer," she says. "We realized we would have to get more organized. We appointed officers, turned a lot of the work over to the women who didn't have babies yet (they had free time and we didn't) and became a non-profit corporation in 1982, a year after my first living-room gathering." She laughs as she recalls sitting at the dining room table organizing the letters into regional areas, connecting the women with each other. "It was manual labor without the Internet [but] it was a lot of fun."

Mattes is careful to point out that they are not advocating that "everyone should go and do this" but rather that single motherhood be viewed as another valid choice. "If you haven't found a man in time, you don't have to go without a family if you don't want to. I encourage women to just explore it."

When I press her about the role of the Women's Movement in the very existence of her organization, she says, "The Women's Movement drives this. Women are having careers. In some cases, they are making as much money as men, enough to support a family. If women can be executives or senators, they can be mothers. Woman without any training have become mothers, it doesn't sound so difficult. The difficult question is: can you do it alone? In our organization they are not doing it alone. Hillary [Clinton] says it takes a village, and she was talking about married women. So it certainly takes a village if you are single."

Around the same time Hillary wrote *It Takes a Village: Other Lessons Children Teach Us*, Mattes wrote:

> The days when a woman had to be married to feel that she could have a rewarding and satisfying life are long over, and women who do not marry have many other ways to find fulfillment . . . marriage is not her only path to happiness.[3]

If it has been a happy path, in the first place. "I hear from my patients all the time: 'my parents went through a bad divorce. *Any* divorce is a bad divorce for children. [These women] are much more realistic about marriage . . . marriage isn't heaven and it's not the answer . . . for children of the '70s and '80s, there was a big peak where everyone who ever wanted to get divorced did; their image of marriage is more realistic. It's no longer the panacea we saw in the movies [where] every thing was 'happily ever after.' All movies ended with the marriage. We never saw what happened after that."

I stop short at this point in the interview and ponder that. I think it is a profound thought that bears repeating: "It all ended with the marriage." *And they all lived happily ever after.* What real lessons could we possibly have garnered from these storybook endings?

HAPPILY. EVER. AFTER. I think about the box of photos I found when I cleaned out my mother's apartment after she died. There are pictures of us as babies. Lots of snapshots of us in the Halloween costumes she sewed. A handful of the holiday table at my grandparents' home: everyone gone now but one aunt and the little boys wearing ties and the daintily-dressed girls. My brothers, cousins and me. At the bottom of the box I see the corner of a picture of my mother in her bridal veil. I pull it out only to discover a long ragged edge where she must have ripped my father from their wedding portrait. To have kept the jagged half, a young woman bedecked on her wedding day, 21 years old and smiling with anticipation, was sadder by far. Happily ever after? I think not.

Over the years, Mattes has heard a number of patients say they married just to have a baby. "And the marriage is miserable," she says, "and then its over." Some tell her they don't want to make a bad marriage and then suffer through a divorce. "Women are now articulating that: 'I don't want to get married just to have a child. I'm not going to do that.' They are protective and caring about the children."

She points out that there is none of the trauma of the broken home in families where a woman chooses to have children alone. Some people question the effect of the absence of a father and assume that the children must have experienced some form of trauma or abandonment issues, "they point to studies about children from 'broken homes,' confusing our families with divorced families. Our homes have not been broken, and out children have not experienced any such trauma."[4]

But becoming a single mother by choice is not a decision to be taken lightly, she councils. Her book outlines the concerns. One of the most pressing issues is financial security. "You cannot responsibly bring a child into the world unless you know you have sufficient money to support the two of you and provide for your basic needs."[5] She encourages mothers to have life insurance, disability and a college fund.

And then there is this: The Daddy Issue. "The subject of what to tell our children about their fathers is by far the biggest concern." She urges women to try and "resolve whatever anger or disappointment you may have about the circumstances of your child's conception before she is old enough to start asking questions."[6] The book also provides practical suggestions for dealing with "Daddy Questions" that might come up at school and in general social interaction ("Everyone has a father, not everyone has a dad") and includes a guide for age-appropriate answers. She examines the father/daddy difference and how to introduce strong male role models.

But by far, the most poignant issue that Mattes explores, and the one that touches me most deeply as I watch women I know who want babies move into their forties childless and disappointed, is what she calls "grieving the dream."

"Some women more, some women less," she says. "Some need to realize they are giving up a dream and in order to move on they really need to address this.

Nobody comes into this 100% resolved." A good therapist helps. "You listen: six more months and six more months . . . OK, this is not going to happen in time. That's the beginning of the grieving."

"I feel very bad for anybody who has to grapple with this, but I feel less bad if they don't grapple with it. Either move forward, or decide that you are not that interested in doing it alone. A lot of women are not ready to grieve the motherhood element until they are in menopause because they are not sure when their fertility will run out until it does . . . having the baby helps because all of a sudden you have this miracle in your arms. Very few people say they would not do it again because they are in love with their babies. Some are sorry they didn't do it sooner."

It is in the "grieving the dream" process where the SMC online forum is most helpful, says Mattes. "There is support for the process of sorting it all out." The forum has sections for fertility issues, pregnancy loss and after pregnancy. There are 'list mamas' who moderate the discussions and most chapters have meetings. "It's pretty lively."

SMC has now been around long enough that there are children who have come up through the organization, including her own son. "So far, so good," says Mattes. We haven't seen any dramatic angst . . . we learned a lot from the adoption world. As a therapist I make a strong case for this: talk about this with the children from the time they are in your arms. I really have pushed all the literature that says openness is best."

With her son about to be married in the coming year, she says, "It is a whole new thing to go through—something I never experienced myself. There are so many more options in the world. There is no one right way. [Women] don't feel the same financial need. What would you do 40 or 50 years ago? Who would take care of you if you weren't married? Therapists in the past told women to be good wives . . . [It was] not an option in the past to live a happy life unless you were married."

I share with Mattes Dr. Claudia Pascale's concern that the amount of choice we have not only presents alternatives and solutions, but its own set of problems. When there are still choices and unexplored options, it's hard to give up. I explain that my research shows this issue is more prevalent in metropolitan areas.

"Life in the city is endless opportunity," she says. "Some people talk about it as an endless department store: you can go from this department to that department and there is always a new department and always new merchandise in each department. If you are in a smaller town, you're kind of limited in your options.

People are not feeling the need to get married. It's happening without the ceremony or the license. They do the things that would come with marriage, like a will, health proxy, domestic partnership. We don't know what [marriage] is going to look like going forward, but the fact that it's so complicated to get out of, people are less excited to get into it."

As for coupling in general, "It's a numbers game amongst hundreds you might go out with once," Mattes explains. "The option is to move ahead in your life. But you need to grieve the dream. If you don't, it is certainly likely to come back and hit you later."

I know I should be happier as I pack up to leave her office, but I am not. I am sad for all the women who were fed the dream of "happily ever after" and angry at myself for not seeing the bitter truth behind the Wizard's curtain, although I was living it every day growing up. I want all these younger women to experience the joys I have known in motherhood. A little hand on a nursing breast. A toddler stroking your hair. The first autonomous "No!" The relief of school starting in September. The joy of welcoming your child home and hearing about her day. The horror of seeing your son elbowed on the basketball court, blood gushing from his mouth, and the relief to see that it is *only* a split lip. All of it. The good, the bad and the ugly.

I want them to experience the sense of accomplishment and completion when a child leaves the nest and successfully goes out on their own. I am convinced in my heart that it is no less, and maybe even more, than the satisfaction Sheryl Sandburg feels when she introduces a new interface or policy at Facebook. *(Did you know that Facebook and Apple will now pay for their female employees to have egg freezing and storage procedures? Now, THAT is a terrific little baby to be proud of.)*

"Once the grieving is faced and done," says Mattes, sensing my distress, "we can be free to more fully enjoy those wonderful aspects of life that we do have: our children, our careers, our friends and family or whatever else we may enjoy. Being single today is not necessarily a lonely existence, nor is it perceived as a sign of failure, as used to be the case." You fill up with other things.

I see that being unmarried and unpregnant is not the end of the world. There is life beyond. Thank you, Jane Mattes.

FIFTEEN

Grieving the Dream

It is July 4th. We are at our home in the woods. It is hot and humid and we have a houseful of people. My daughter is here with her chubby pug Nugget and a friend from the city who is ensconced with one of the *Game of Thrones* books on the blowup mattress in the basement. My younger son and his fiancé are encamped in the yellow bedroom, backs against the headboard with laptops on their stomachs as they both work. The expectant couple is upstairs with their dog, an aging Japanese Chin who would be 98 in people years.

I am alone in the kitchen getting breakfast ready, preparing to bake cookies. I have already been to the garden and collected mint for tea and checked the progress of the tomato plants bursting with the promise of a handful of ripe Sweet 100s by the end of the weekend. The morning unfolds. This one comes in for a cup of coffee. That one snags a bottle of water from the fridge. My husband is doing *something* in the garage, which often consists of moving boxes and paint cans to a new location. I have not seen the married couple yet.

When my son finally comes into the kitchen, he looks distressed. He is carrying a small, full garbage bag and is looking for another.

"What's up?" I say.

"I think we're miscarrying," he answers. He gestures with

the plastic garbage bag, offering it as proof. His hazel eyes are dark. His lip trembles.

I go to sit in a chair at the kitchen table. I do not know what to say.

"We may have to go to the hospital," he says. "We are waiting to hear from the doctor."

"What can I do?" I ask.

He shakes his head sadly. This is their second pregnancy, second loss.

"Nothing."

An hour later he knocks on our bedroom door, where I have retreated to await whatever happens next.

"Can you drive us to the hospital?"

"Of course. Let me get my keys."

"Don't tell the others. We don't want to spoil their day."

"I have to say something."

"Just say she has a really bad stomachache. Food poisoning."

I take my daughter-in-law's elbow as she moves slowly down the stairs and into the car. She is bent double from severe cramping. Her distinctive long lashes are damp, and there are gray shadows beneath her eyes, remnants of makeup. She looks up at me but looks away quickly, not sure which one of us will break first. She knows my investment in this grandchild. We have shared the weekly countdown.

At the emergency room, the staff is kind except for the idiot hematologist who tries to take her blood with an adult-sized needle. My daughter-in-law is tiny. Her hands are tiny and I am sure her veins are tiny. I tell the guy he needs to use a child-sized needle. He ignores me and sticks her multiple times with a full-sized needle and moves it around, looking to connect with her blood. It doesn't work. She has never been in a hospital before, never had a medical procedure. He is creating trauma where it doesn't need to be. I request a nurse or supervisor.

"Moron," I pronounce as he leaves the room.

"Jackass," my son counters.

My daughter-in-law is as white as the sheets she is pressing into.

A nurse comes in and looks at her punctured arm. She selects a child's needle and the blood sample is complete before I have finished making my complaint.

All the vitals are done and the doctor on call shoos us from the room to do her examination. We wait outside the curtain. Then we wait together in the room, my middle son, his wife and me, for a call from her obstetrician.

There is no more baby. We know this from the faces around us before her doctor calls to confirm it. We wait several more hours in the emergency room to make sure the shedding of the uterine lining is progressing as it should. Nobody talks much.

I call home and update my husband. I tell him to let the others know. First he must tell them my daughter-in-law was pregnant. Then he must tell them she is not.

It has been over five hours. They discharge us and send us on our way for my daughter-in-law to continue the process at home. No one has eaten. We stop at a diner where we all order lightly. They sit on one side of the booth; my daughter-in-law leans heavily into my son's side. His arm fully encompasses her shoulders. I feel his protection as I sit across from them, witnessing their pain. I see his lip tremble again. This is not a man who cries and he is struggling.

I try to think of something to offer up. "There will be others." "You can try again." These are stupid platitudes, offered up by the most well-meaning of people. I know this for a fact. I have been on the receiving end. But then something profound occurs to me.

I am sitting at this table, with my child who is now a grown man. He is grieving the child he was hoping to have. It is *this* child of mine, this man that I love and admire for his strength, his stability and his noble way of thinking, who would not be here if I had not lost my second baby. If I had not recovered and moved forward after the stillbirth of my second daughter, Jillian, I would not be here now with my son, being strong for him. Oh, the world has a cruel sense of irony.

I look at his face, his full lips, and I can see Jillian. Her rosebud mouth was full and pursed, just like his at birth. Only her lips were black. I only know this because the delivery room nurse was well-schooled in the practices of neo-natal grief and healing.

"You should hold her," she said to me as I came out from the haze of anesthesia.

"Why?" I asked. "She's dead."

"Because one day you may be sorry that you didn't know her." So I did. I took the warm little bundle the nurse offered me and gazed at her face, as though looking at a doll. Despite myself, I touched her cheek.

"She's warm," I said, as though they might have made a mistake. "Why is she warm?"

"For just this reason. So you can hold her." These babies are kept in an incubator until parents are ready to see them. I did not know for many years that my husband had already done this.

"It was a cord accident," the doctor told me later that day. "Three times wrapped around her neck and pulled up between her legs." He cried with me at my bedside, helpless to offer anything more. I think of that doctor now and remember his compassion.

I look at my son across the Formica tabletop. He and his wife are brokenhearted.

"You are here, because she isn't," I say. "And I wouldn't wish you away to have her for even a moment. You will have a baby—a healthy baby," I tell both of them. "And that will be the baby who was meant to be."

Maybe I put too much stock in Fate. Or the Universe. Or God—whatever you conceive that to be. But I am a believer in the rightness of things. Or our ability to readjust our thinking and find the rightness so that we can go on. And often in the world at large and sometimes in our personal lives, it isn't right. And it isn't fair. And we have to go on anyway. What are our choices? So we grieve the loss and push forward.

SIXTEEN

Been There, Done That

It is just what I had always imagined: the day dawns bright and clear after a night of summer rain. Sunlight glistens on the very tips of the grass where raindrops linger; droplets pool in the upturned faces of the roses that intertwine with morning glories along the fence. The humidity has dropped, the air is fresh and dry. A perfect day for a wedding.

It is three years before the miscarriage. We all gather for breakfast but no one eats much. The anticipation fills us up. We pass *The New York Times* around, exchanging sections of the Sunday paper. I sip my tea. We make small talk and big talk about the meaning of the day. Who will be there, who is gone. We reminisce.

After breakfast, the boys make themselves scarce while my daughter and I fuss over every little detail. Something old, something new, something borrowed . . . something blue. We have no clue how blue. The hairdresser arrives. The photographer. My daughter's BFF stylist who tapes my breasts together and sews me into my gown at the last minute because I have actually lost too much weight over the previous week anticipating this day. *(Honey, these hands have taped Kristin Chenoweth's breasts. Now drop your dress!)* The room vibrates like a bee hive.

My daughter steps into her crinoline. Her dress. I zip her up. She looks like a princess. Her pale skin is flushed. Her hands tremble slightly and her once-bitten nails, now manicured to perfection, fiddle with the diamond ring she wears. A beautiful bride. As it should be.

The limo arrives to ferry us to the venue. Everyone is chattering and fussing with their hair and makeup, electric with excitement. It is a short ride and we are there in no time. The chauffeur extends an arm and guides each of us out of the ridiculously long vehicle. We stand up straight and fluff our dresses. We surround the bride, admiring her and each other. Then one by one we proceed through the huge double doors, past a soaring round lobby and into the vast hall. The lights are dimmed. It is magical. The flowers we have agonized and compromised over—I wanted sweet, dainty and romantic, she wanted heavy, dark and gothic—are spectacular. Like walking into an enchanted forest. Little tea lights sparkle from within the greenery. Burgundy amaranth clusters drape low between poufy antique hydrangeas. A piano plays somewhere in the distance. Perfect.

The ceremony proceeds with just the right amount of comic relief: just as my dead mother's name is summoned for remembrance on this special day, a huge tray of dishes crashes to the floor beyond the curtained wall where they are readying the cocktail area. That, too, is perfect *(she loved to be the center of attention)*. The party is sumptuous, but we forget to eat. We dance with abandon, surrounded by all the people we love and even some family members we don't. And that, too, is just perfect. Perfect. Perfect. It is everything I have ever wanted in a wedding. What a shame the marriage is wrong.

It is over in six weeks. The lying bastard has somehow forgotten to share his full criminal record and nasty cocaine addiction with my beautiful and brokenhearted daughter. Oh, the one arrest for possession? We know all about *that.* That is a forgivable offense for the young and careless. It is the dozens of *other* arrests that are hard to swallow. And the stalking charge scares the shit out of me. But it doesn't behoove anyone for me to talk about it. I will let her tell you in her own words, which she has so generously agreed to do.

"I always assumed I would, at some point, get married. I think it was implied," my daughter says. "I thought I would be starring on Broadway, living in a loft in Manhattan with a man who vaguely resembled the Ken doll who came wearing a suit with suspenders. I was technically only married for six weeks and it was not like any marriage ever should be," she says. "But until the shit actually hit the fan I was ok with it because I thought that when you loved someone and they loved you, the momentary happiness wasn't the point; the 'creating a good life together' was. And if we could support each other through the hard times it would mean we would have great good times."

And live happily ever after?

The "shit that hit the fan" was her discovery that her drug addicted husband was depositing stolen money in their joint bank account, among other offenses.

But she has no regrets. "I would not wish any of that to happen to anyone. And I feel horrible about the impact that it had on my friends and family. However, the person I have grown into and the things that I have done since, I don't think would have been possible without this struggle. And I love my life right now so I can't regret the path I took to get here."

When I press her to elaborate on that path, she shares things I didn't know. I find them sad, touching and illuminating.

"I started dating my would-be husband because, after my

grandmother died, I thought it would be better to be in any relationship than to be alone. I had been told that while she lay dying she waited just long enough to have her asshole of a husband with her, holding her hand, and then she died." (Note from Mom: that would be the second husband. The one who gave all her money away to a Nigerian internet scheme in hopes of inheriting $20 million from a relative he didn't know he had.)

"I decided that I didn't want to die alone. I remember telling a friend of mine, the next week, that I was finally ready and was going to be in a relationship very soon. And then I was. He was far from perfect on paper—no steady job, no college degree, not Jewish, smoked cigarettes. But he liked me. And he made an effort to make me happy. And we liked the same movies. And while he didn't have a steady job he was Grammy-nominated for his work . . . so we started dating and then quickly moved in together because neither one of us wanted to spend nights apart," She says.

"The truth is, getting married was never a priority or even a specific want for me. When I told my best friend from childhood that I was getting married she was surprised that I agreed. I always felt that if I found someone I loved and he loved me I didn't need a big show. But it was important to him and so I thought it would be nice. My other grandmother had just passed away after a long fight with brain cancer and I thought it would be good for my family to have something happy to celebrate together."

She continues: "Thanks almost entirely to my mother, I had a beautiful wedding. And thanks in large part to me, a shitty marriage. What did I learn? I learned that if I tell people

I'm happy, they believe me. And that is not good enough. I know now, without question, that being alone for the right reasons is better than being with someone for the wrong ones. My last boyfriend also was bad on paper and even though he had the most wonderful redeeming traits, when he couldn't support me, I broke it off. I didn't feel the same need to make it work. I know that I am supposed to be in a relationship. But I will not try to force another square peg into a round hole. I still am not sure what the right relationship looks like but I am always on the lookout for the signs of the wrong one. So, I am equally willing to have more first dates and less second ones. I know the game, I know the rules now. I just have to figure out how to win. But even as I write that, I am conflicted, because I don't see getting married or finding a man as winning. But isn't it? If I can be happy and married, then that's what I want. If it's one or the other, I choose happy. In the conversation when I told my husband it was over, I said 'you put me in a position where I have to choose you or me and I choose me.' Maybe the right relationship is the one where the choice is between us and me. In which case I hope I do choose us," she reasons.

"I would love to . . . have someone who is inherently on my team and I'm on theirs. What I have learned is that I don't want to settle . . . and that I am completely fine on my own. I only want the relationship that complements both people involved. My brothers are the role models for what I know is possible in a partner. And unlike the last time, I won't pretend a relationship is something other than what it is. And if I am being completely honest with myself, it's very important. At Rosh Hashana every year Jews say, 'Next year in Jerusalem.' On my birthday each year I say quietly to myself, 'next year in a relationship.'"

She got rid of his stuff and sold the ring she was still paying off on their joint credit card. Bruised but undaunted, she hopes to marry again. But “I will approach it more like a business transaction,” she says. “Love is great and wanting to spend your life with someone is wonderful. Marriage is a contract and is not to be taken lightly or without the appropriate emotionless due diligence required to make a responsible choice.”

And then there is motherhood. As she approaches her mid thirties and I become more annoying and anxious in my desire for a grandchild, she is level-headed. “I think it’s mostly biological—wanting to be a caretaker, passing on my family values and contributing a good human to the world,” says my daughter. “Being pregnant is an important part of being a mother to me. I am not sure I would go a way that doesn’t involve that.” So much for all those great contacts I have made in the fertility world.

Testing my thesis out on my own kid, I ask her if she thinks feminism has empowered her. “Given who I am and what I do—being a woman in finance—I sometimes think I must be one. But then I read Sheryl Sandberg’s *Lean In* and think feminism is a bunch of women whining about things being unfair instead of just showing up, doing the work and taking on life as it comes. There is discrimination everywhere to just about everyone. Making a cause and calling yourself a victim without taking the actions to follow through on change is a waste of time.” I tell her she is able to think that *because of* feminism. No, she replies. “It’s just how I was raised.” I rest my case.

***

You met Melanie earlier in this book. She and her mother, Barbara, were both open to sharing how Barbara's brief marriage and chaotic upbringing took a toll on both their lives and attitudes toward marriage and children. Melanie has had her own brief marriage.

The second child of her parents' first marriage, she also has two brothers and two sisters from her father's second marriage and another sister from his third marriage. She is 40; her youngest sibling is 16.

Melanie specifically remembers her mother telling her to "have a career first. Learn who you are first and then see if you want the rest. That getting married is bad deal for women and you should be independent." She understands now that much of what her mother accomplished was "done out of a need to be a good parent. The professional accomplishments and the money she earned was so that she could provide a good life for us." She didn't have much choice as Barbara left her husband when she was five months pregnant with Melanie. "Their divorce was *The War of the Roses*," Melanie says. "My father was horrible to her for years after their divorce and she fought him every step of the way."

She acknowledges that her father was "frustrated, angry and unhappy . . . he would get melancholy . . . he enjoyed the excitement [and] challenges of his work but hated the boredom of it and imparted that he wanted me to be able to set my own schedule and not be at the whim of a boss . . . my father was wealthy, but spent much of his money on lawyers and court fees fighting my mother . . . [he] had more children, spent more money and didn't continue to innovate as he had done in his youth and so he went from being wealthy to middle class," she says. "When I was twelve I thought I would never get married because it seemed like a bad idea and I didn't want kids. I felt that way for a long time."

Despite her bad introduction to marriage, Melanie *did* marry. She was 29. "It was a green-card wedding," she explains. "We loved each other, but it certainly wasn't any kind of mature love. I had been in a lesbian relationship for five years and he was my rebound. I was living in Europe and wanted to come back to America to get my master's degree and he wanted to come with me, so we got married. He was way too young for me. He was an alcoholic or rather became an alcoholic or I realized he was an alcoholic after we were married . . . he hated New York and he hated the Midwest, and we were miserable. I had spent all my of my twenties in committed relationships—five years with a woman and five years with a man—and I was deeply unhappy." Melanie and her husband separated. He went back to Europe and she completed her education and founded a small company. But she would still like to meet someone."

She says that she's lonely. "I have sex basically, *never*. I don't date because I don't meet anyone who interests me who is single. I sense that I missed the boat somehow . . . married men often try to pick me up and it makes me think there is something about me that is flawed compared to the women they are committed to or married to, who they nevertheless obviously cheat on."

Despite these feelings of inadequacy and longing, Melanie has created a very full life for herself. "I work 12-18 hours a day on average. I love my friends and my career is starting to take off. Now when I see the sun on the horizon, I would like to share that with a person. I would like to have sex a few times a week instead of a few times a year and I would like to have a family . . . I didn't actually start wanting children until I was divorced . . . I still would like to think I have some time left to make it happen . . . but I probably don't."

She is holding out hope to become a mother by natural means. "I'm not in a place where I am willing to consider that it won't happen yet. I want to believe I still have that option. Maybe I'm kidding myself, but I see plenty of women in their early forties in New York who have kids, so it seems like it may still be a possibility."

What about a relationship? Without a doubt, she tells me, but there is a codicil. "I've been alone for nearly a decade. Am I willing to be with someone I don't love? NO. I've been unhappy in relationships before and I would rather be unhappy alone than unhappy and lonely and have to share my home or bed with someone I don't love. But yes, it's really important and it sucks that I can't find it."

Jessie is 30 years old. She grew up in Kansas City, the daughter of a Filipino nurse and Caucasian father, who was very present when she was growing up. Her father started law school when Jessie was three and her mother helped to pay for it.

"It was almost as if he were a stay-at-home dad," she says. "He was always the one who could take off work to chaperone a field trip, or follow my various sports teams all around the country to watch me play. The running joke was that to find my dad, just follow the extension cord connected to his laptop, but he was always there."

Jessie's mother enjoyed her work so much she waited until she was 32 to have Jessie and gave birth to her son at 40. Her mother had a very distinct and traditional plan for Jessie. She wanted to "find me an older man with money so I would always be taken care of. While I was in high school, she was continually trying to set me up with resident doctors at the hospital where she worked . . . she always made it very clear that the expectation was to settle down and begin my own family."

And Jessie cooperated. She started dating her almost-husband at 16. "We moved in together when I was 17 (right after I graduated high school) and got engaged when I was 18 . . . his parents were high school sweethearts . . . and I think are still married. He was your typical small town, all-American, star athlete boy. He was very close with his parents and his brothers . . . in fact, the house we lived in and the house that his older brother and sister-in-law lived in were all on his parents' property. My engagement was definitely not what I thought it was going to be. Looking back, I was super naïve . . . it was not all hearts and rainbows. Somehow, I envisioned this very happy, floating on clouds, doing everything together engagement. Instead, it was a lot of bickering that lead to self-growth; unfortunately, each of our growth was done individually and not together . . . which led to more fighting and doubt." The relationship started going downhill.

Jessie has spent many hours trying to analyze what went wrong, aside from being just too young. She has broken it down for me:

"Issue 1: I wasn't 21 yet. He was. So as he was out drinking and gambling, I was out with my other under-aged friends drinking at house parties . . . or waiting for him to come home.

Issue 2: Later that year, I seriously injured myself doing something stupid, and his response was that I 'deserved' it. As

I was home on bed rest, needing help even going to the bathroom and showering, my emotional state started to deteriorate: self-pity, anger, depression. We fought about this constantly. Eventually, he went out more and more and was home less and less." They broke off the engagement ten months into it. "It was definitely not what I thought it was going to be.

"As I began to recover, our relationship was already strained. We started going out separately and growing even further apart (we both harbored extreme resentment towards each other). One night I didn't come home. I stayed with one of my male friends. Admittedly, he and I slept in the same bed, [but there was] no physical or sexual contact. I blamed it on drinking and knowing I shouldn't drive home; the truth was I didn't *want* to go home. For the first time in months, I felt wanted by someone of the opposite sex . . . without having to have sex," She explains.

"I was honest with him about where I stayed. The next day he put all of my belongings in yellow trash bags . . . put them on our front porch and called my dad to pick me up. It was over."

Like my daughter, Jessie says she has no regrets. "Though, that's not to say I don't look back and wonder what my life would have been if I hadn't gotten drunk and gotten hurt." And she is guarded about the idea of marriage in the future.

"For the past 10 years, I've completely bashed the idea of marriage. My paternal grandfather left my grandmother for another woman when my dad was very young. They have been happily together ever since, and never legally married. I always cited their relationship as evidence that being "married" was never a pre-requisite for happiness. It hasn't been until recently that the thought of getting married has not made my stomach turn." Fair enough. There is plenty of evidence that marriage is not necessarily the answer.

How about future relationships, however you define them? "As one of my close friends has pointed out to me, I live life to win. I will analyze and pick situations apart until I know exactly how the game is played," she says. "And then I will crush my opponent. I will win. Sadly, it turns into the same thing in a relationship. I will crave the emotional aspect of another person, but as soon as it gets too emotional or starts going a little sideways, I will turn it into a game. And I will win it. So to combat this, I continually get into relationships that I know going in have an expiration date. And I will be the one who ends it. I win."

It is interesting to note that both Jessie and my daughter use the term "to win" when talking about relationships. As if it were a competition. Or a game. As if there were a set of rules somewhere that, if followed precisely, would take you down the yellow brick road or the rose strewn carpet to "Happily Ever After." Or Oz. Ain't no such book, ladies. Ain't no such place.

I ask Jessie if children figure into her future. "I go back and forth on this one. The idea of children, especially having my own children, terrifies me. At this point in my life, it's not important to me at all. I have a plan for my life and my career. Nowhere in that plan does it include children; in fact, I worry that having children may derail those plans. Perhaps this will change down the road (I'm guessing when I feel like I've accomplished my goals) . . . I used to joke that I wanted to get married to a man who had his own grown children, so that I could bypass being a mother and skip straight to being a grandmother. This, in fact, may not be the best alternative way to become a parent."

***

I've got one more "Been There, Done That" for you. Emily. Exotic, blonde, non-conformist Emily. An only child, born in Los Angeles when her mother was 35 and her father was 28.

"I learned more about family from my father," Emily jumps right into the conversation. "My mother was more my friend than parent, and my dad raised me to prioritize the family that *acts* like one over blood lines. Family is to be appreciated and the relationships shouldn't be taken for granted. I learned a lot about parenting from my dad's parenting style, and it's in part because he took the role so seriously that I know I am not in a position to, or interested in, having children." Well, that solves that. No grandchildren coming any time soon from *this* 32-year-old.

What was it about her father, who passed away several years ago, that was such a significant influence? I want to know if he was a happy man. "Very," she says. "For the most part, I'd say he was happy or thought he was happy until he realized he wasn't. He was constantly seeking love, happiness and family. He got happier after he and my mother split and he began being more honest about who he was and living that truth."

He taught Emily "that hard work is everything. Nothing will be handed to me—I have to earn things, especially as a woman it was important to him that I learn to be self-sufficient."

She goes on the discuss how her family imparted goals to

her. "My parents raised me to seek truth and happiness, whatever that meant for me. I was on a path to be in the theater, and that is the path I followed from age nine through going to an arts high school all the way through starting as a theater major in New York, the real end goal. As for 'family' in the 'you grow up, you get married, you have kids' sense: that was never the point or purpose or end goal of my life. Did my parents want me to be happy and find love with a partner? Absolutely. But it was always more important to be a good person and spend my time with good people who care about me."

She feels that she has, indeed followed that path. "I came to New York and after a series of events, found my way back to performing. Of course, it didn't happen in an expected way, but after 14 years of living in New York I am doing what I set out to: perform." She is now a well-known personality in alternative theater.

Emily is proud of her accomplishments and has a sanguine approach to her short-lived marriage. "I never intended to get married so I never had any expectations of what it would be. I assumed that being married was like not being married but with a legal document, and for the most part it was. Although I will say that something intangible definitely changes in a relationship once you actually get married. I'm not sure what, or why, but it's undeniable.

"When I saw my parents separate as a kid, I decided then and there I didn't want to get married. I always felt that if a relationship that is important enough to make you want to get married ends, then adding having to take care of business and legal issues while you're also in the process of mourning the loss of your partner and relationship seemed like an extra painful and unnecessary stress. It seemed to me that being in love should be enough. I got married for insurance purposes, and while we were in love when we made that decision, neither my now ex-husband or I had intended to marry until that need became apparent." She explains there were many factors that contributed to the marriage ending, "most of which probably stem from the fact that in the six years we were together, I really learned who I am, and *that* person couldn't fully thrive and develop in the context of our relationship. Marriages succeed when couples change together or in compliment of each other; I was changing and in the entire time we were together, my ex didn't change at all."

Emily says, "as I began to discover myself, I did try to keep our relationship together, but as I was starting to identify my needs and ask for things, he would listen to me, but his behavior didn't change in the way I needed it to. I've learned a lot about what I need in a partner from that relationship, and since, and knowing what I know now, my ex simply couldn't be the person I need in a partner, and I am not who he needs in a partner, either."

And motherhood is just not in the picture at this time. "I don't see why it should be important to me to be a mother. There are more than enough people on the planet, my cousins have all taken care of carrying on the bloodline, and I don't feel a deep need to have my own children as some do. I think I've always been heading toward alternate paths. That said, I recently came to realize that among the reasons why I have always said I want to be 'fun aunt' and not 'mom' was because I believe parenting is a selfless and full-time job. I have very high standards for parents, standards that at this time in my life, I'm both not interested in and not capable of upholding. However, if I met the right person and was in the right position financially, with my career, and with my partner, I'm not opposed to the idea of having children."

It is amazing to me how *women* feel the need to justify their choices about motherhood. Am I a bad person—bad woman—if I don't want kids? *Wait!* Maybe if I met the right partner . . . if I had enough money . . . the right career. Did we not convey the message that it's okay not to *want* children? Probably not, I surmise.

I ask Emily what differences she sees between her mother's life and her own, both of them married and divorced, and her answer is insightful. "I actually think that, completely inadvertently, our lives are more similar than different. My mom had me late; she hadn't intended on having children either, and only did because she met my dad. She pursued her career and her social interests, and she valued friendships and her family (mother, father, siblings, grandparents) before having me. I'm still four years younger than my mom was when she had me. A lot can happen and change in four years, and without meaning to follow in my mom's footsteps, so far my life path sort of has."

But still. *But still.* "I'd like to find a partner," Emily says. "I do not need to be in a relationship, but I would like to love and be loved."

My daughter gets rid of her wedding china, strips the apartment of all reminders of her ex. My son sells his sister's wedding dress on Craigslist. I keep my strapless gown in the back of the closet. It is the most beautiful dress I have ever worn. I can't wear it again—I can barely look at it—but I can't throw it away. I have one small album of wedding photos tucked away in a box in the basement. Dreams die hard.

SEVENTEEN

Divorce and Damage

Divorce? What is a chapter about divorce doing in a book that is mostly about women who haven't even been carried over the threshold yet? Because we need to talk about it. It's pertinent. I am, for the most part, not talking about *their* divorces. I went there and did that in *Been There, Done That*. I am talking about their parents' divorces. I am talking about battlegrounds that should have been safe havens and role models that should have inspired emulation instead of the opposite. I am a full generation ahead of these women, but I think my experience is relevant. I remember sitting in an Outback restaurant in Florida having a conversation with my father, a WWII vet with unresolved issues whom I had not seen in many years, in the only terms he could understand.

I tell him that his relationship with my mother was never my war. We, the children may have become embroiled in certain skirmishes—like the time my older brother wrestled a knife out of my father's hand when he was threatening our mother—but it wasn't our battle. We didn't lie, or cheat or steal money. We did not commit offenses against either of our parents, at least not in that adult way that created the rift between them. We were the innocent bystanders, splattered with shrapnel. We were the witnesses to their personal jihad.

I cannot speak for either of my brothers. They have wrestled their demons on their own terms. The older one has waged a lifelong battle with addiction. He has been stoned beyond function, also clean and sober and a national advocate for AA. The younger one has had, perhaps a more subtle struggle, but difficult nonetheless. His enemy has been the past and our mother's indiscretions and his attempt to hold at bay the backwash, barricading it from the satisfying life he has built as an adult. But we are survivors. Against all odds, we are three people who endured a violent, dysfunctional childhood and have gone on to make long term marriages of 40, 38 and 34 years. It has not always been easy, we have paid the piper along the way, but it is nonetheless remarkable, considering the damage we sustained.

My father does not understand this. In his ninetieth year, he continues to rage against my mother, who has been dead for six years, and by association, me, because I am a woman who at times aligned with her. But I continue to believe I am among the innocent. I am a casualty of *their* war, triumphant only because of the wonderful therapists and supportive husband I was lucky to find.

Divorce is a malignant disease that affects the fabric of families for generations forward. I have heard my own children reference my difficult childhood with a mixture of reverence and pity for how it has shaped me and my parenting. *(I can be tough. Hard. A softy: I cry easily.)* Hence: how it affects them.

I remember one particular holiday: we were all sitting around my mother's dining room table. However real or imagined the catalyst, bitter or benign, she let loose a barrage of words aimed at annihilating me. In front of our guests, my husband and our children. One by one, the kids got out of their chairs and came to stand behind me, each placing a hand on my shoulder. The oldest could not have been more than nine. As tears crested in my eyes, a mixture of pain and embarrassment, I became aware that they were aligned there, a wall of defense against her unwarranted attack. I have built this fortress, I thought. I have broken the cycle.

There are times they know they must "pussyfoot" around me, occasions when they circumvent me entirely to avoid my emotional backpack *(it used to be a steamer trunk)* and deal directly with their father. For the most part, on the functional surface, he is the product of a model "Leave It To Beaver" upbringing. It is not lost on me how my parents' divorce has resonated in my children's lives; as well as a traumatized mother, they inherited sometimes hurtful, often absent grandparents. It pains me that my parents have missed so much joy.

Leapfrog a generation forward. My contemporaries and our parents exhibited the highest divorce rate ever. Blame it on the Women's Movement. Blame it on the sexual revolution, which people blame on the Women's Movement. It doesn't matter. Assign blame where you will. I am concerned with the fallout on the children of these marriages and how it affects their own ability to couple. How about some statistics?[1]

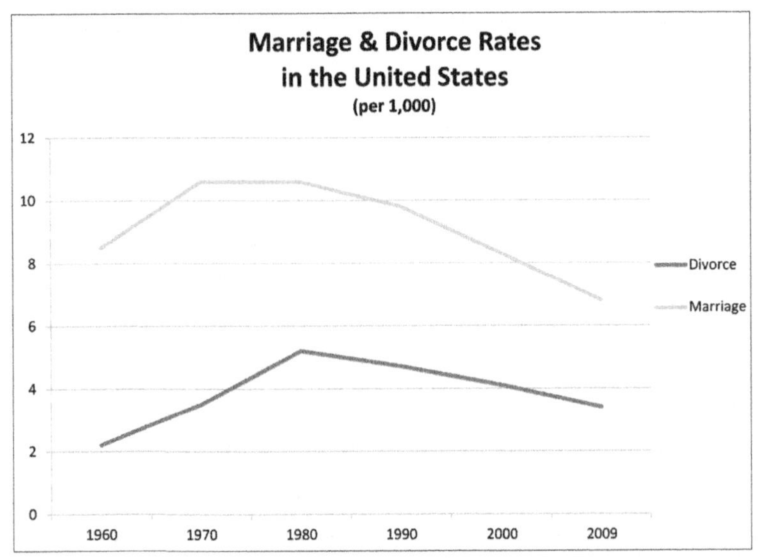

It is a curious finding that the divorce rate very closely mimics the marriage rate. This new century has less folks marrying. Less folks needing a divorce. For a more specific picture, look at the following chart, which breaks down the divorce rate by state.

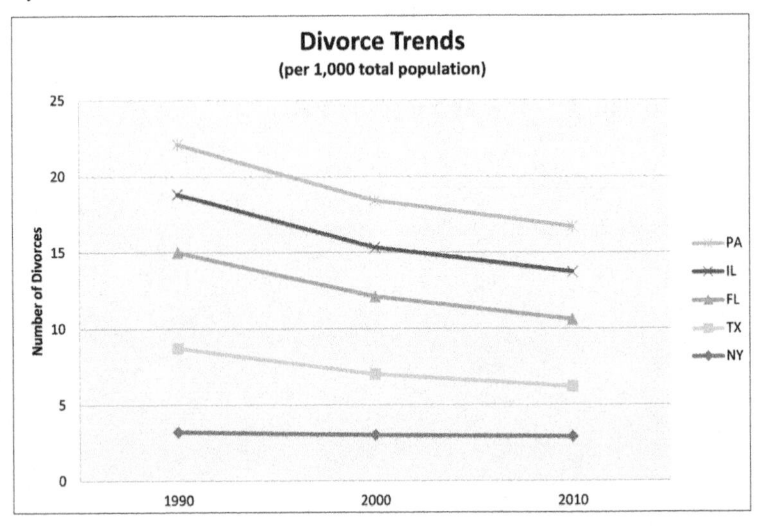

I chose only a few states to illustrate the difference between those that have large, densely populated metropolitan areas and those that don't. In the states with large cities, individuals marry later and have children later. It is interesting to note that New York has had a lower number and more stable rate of divorces over the past 20 years, where there has been a sharp decline in other states.

This is a good time to throw into the mix the stats for those who have never married.

Percent of Persons Who Have Never Married by Sex and Age, 1970, 2000, and 2008

	1970	2000	2008
WOMEN			
15-19	88	94	98
20-24	36	69	80
25-29	12	38	48
30-34	7	22	28
35 and older	7	8	10
Total	**21**	**24**	**28**
MEN			
15-19	96	96	99
20-24	56	79	89
25-29	20	49	61
30-34	11	30	37
35 and older	7	11	13
Total	**26**	**30**	**35**

Look at the numbers for 1970 and 2008 in the category of women 25-29 years old, prime marrying age. There has been a mind-blowing drop from 12% unmarried in 1970 to 48% unmarried in 2008. Take a look at the men's stats in that age group, as well: 20% unmarried in 1970, 61% unmarried in 2008. Let's lay that over the divorce statistics and see the correlation. A drop in both numbers doesn't indicate causality, but it certainly is a disturbing coincidence. ***Something*** happened. And it changed the landscape forever.

I can research and interview until I am blue in the face, but the numbers tell the story of something significant changing a pattern that has been constant for generations. All fingers point to the change in the status of women. The freedom to exit bad marriages or to not enter into marriage at all has created a seismic shift in the American family.

It was foretold. I find the following to be a remarkable statement and **I have put it in bold** because I don't want you to miss it. In 1970, Germaine Greer, wrote in *The Female Eunuch*:

> **The opponents of female suffrage lamented that women's emancipation would mean the end of marriage, morality and the state; their extremism was more clear-sighted than the woolly benevolence of liberals and humanists, who thought that giving women a measure of freedom would not upset anything. When we reap the harvest which the unwitting suffragettes sowed we shall see that the antifeminists were right after all.**[2]

It has not proven to be as extreme as she predicted; I don't think we are experiencing an "end to morality and the state." But oh my, she is quoting *opponents* of the female suffrage movement, which began in the 1840s. That's a very long time ago. And now marriage rates are down. And the birth rate is down. And I still don't have a grandchild.

EIGHTEEN

The Last Rescue

There's an old joke that goes like this:

So there's this huge flood one day, and an entire town looks like it's going to be swallowed up by the waters. The police are running all over the place trying to get people to safety.

They send a rescue boat over to a house where there's a guy sitting on the roof with the water lapping around his ankles. "Come on, quick! Get in. There isn't much time."

"Nah," he says. "It's ok, God will provide."

About an hour later, they're zooming past in the boat again and they see the guy is still there, only the water's up to his waist, almost at the top of the roof.

"Quick!" they say, "Get in the boat, it's gonna get worst before it gets better."

"Nah, don't worry. God will provide."

Finally, a rescue helicopter flies over the area and notices the guy, who is standing on the peak of the roof now, with only his head and shoulders out of the water.

"GRAB THE ROPE!" they cry. "IT'S YOUR ONLY HOPE!"

"Don't worry," he replies calmly "God will provide."

So he drowns. When he gets to heaven he is a little ticked off with God for letting him die.

"I had faith, I believed in you—and still you didn't help me."

"HELP YOU?!" God replies "What MORE did you want. I sent you two boats and a helicopter!"

GET IN THE BOAT, ALREADY!

Meet Amber. She is 42. Blonde hair, blue eyes and drop-dead California gorgeous. We get together for lunch in Manhattan, where she is a high-level executive in the fashion industry. She got there the old fashioned way. She *worked* for it.

"I moved to the city to be an actress," she says. "I met a guy in a pizza shop who offered me a job. I worked part-time [while auditioning] and they trained me in IT. Years later, I met that guy's daughter who hired me full-time. I looked just like his daughter. It was so weird. It changed the fate of my career." And that career has taken her all over the world and right up the corporate ladder, yet she is still surprised to find herself where she is.

"I would see these women who worked in my division—triple threats *(a descriptive industry term left over from her theater days)*: beautiful, accomplished, great personality and people skills. They work in an image-based industry. They are all single. I just never thought that I would be one of them. Ever."

I feel my heartstring reverberate for this charming, beautiful, accomplished woman who is herself a *triple threat*, and we haven't even ordered our salads yet. What she says next blows me away. I think that maybe it's the answer I have been looking for through all my conversations with the professionals and the single women.

"I think there is a niche of us who kind of got caught between our mother's emancipation and women's lib. You know," she says *(and I think I do)* "Our mothers going out into the workforce and doing it all, especially the moms who were single mothers: raising kids, working, doing *everything*, as opposed to the women who I see today who are very much about getting what they want.

Because I was in that gap, I probably focused more on working and doing a job. I had a serious bout of 'workaholism' [and] I was curious and hungry and wanted to learn so much, to do a good job. I kind of missed out on taking care of my health. I think I overdid it. I saw women who were a few years older than me plowing through in the corporate world, as a priority for the first time, having that career."

Reflecting on current youth, "when I see a Millennial *(she snaps out the demographic with disdain)* working for me now, it's so annoying with the snapchatting. I am talking about an Ivy League MBA who is more concerned about her social life and what her gain can be than what she can do for the company or her career. It's about what she can get, dating the guys who make a lot of money and can buy [her] a house *(I think of Stonehill's BBD—Bigger and Better Deal)*. If these women want kids, they should freeze their eggs NOW. Do it, do it, do it!" she exclaims.

So let's back up a bit. She didn't get to this place in *(or with)* a vacuum. "My mom was a feminist in her own right," Amber says. "She was the first one in our town to get divorced." They lived in an upscale part of a suburban Maryland town, in the country club neighborhood. Her mother wanted the divorce but quickly felt ostracized by club members. Even Amber and her two sisters saw friends pull away. It left her feeling stigmatized: "We all felt the shame of it."

But it wasn't completely negative. "In seventh grade health class, a teacher sent me to the office to pick up something. When I was out of the room on this fake task, the teacher told the classroom about the divorce. She told them to be nice. A few months later, a good friend told me her parents were also getting a divorce and we had an instant bond. She was from the other side of town. We are still good friends." Unhappy families know no class distinction.

Amber's mother never seemed to fully recover from the divorce. "I don't think Mom was happy. She never remarried." Her mother recently retired from a career as a drug and alcohol crisis counselor and moved to an apartment. "Her health has declined dramatically," Amber says.

And her dad? "My father remarried a cold woman. She is innately mean and nasty and bosses him around. I have a relationship with her, but she's not nice. She's controlling. She makes dad choose between us and the grandkids (her sisters' children) and her. But he was always very proud of my accomplishments: school president, honor roll, in the plays. Now he is proud and surprised at how well I have done . . . but I often feel—what am I, my resume? He wants me to upgrade my living situation, buy an apartment, to have a better place to invite people over."

Expectations play a large part in Amber's story, as does luck and circumstance. No different from the thousands of stories of women I might meet on the streets of any big city these days.

"College was implied . . . you graduate college, get married, have kids: that's what's expected. That's the normal thing. I moved to the city and the plan kind of changed. [It became] go to college, *get a job* and get married. Then it changed again to add get an MBA, *then* get married and have kids and meet your husband there . . . it was more about career and education once I moved to city. The family piece kind of fell to the wayside, despite that being the template I was raised with, even though my mom worked from the time I was 10."

So why begin this chapter with the joke? Because Amber

has had three proposals. Count 'em: one, two, *three*! And are you sorry you didn't say yes to one of them, I ask, as I imagine that empty rescue helicopter flying off into the vast stormy sky.

"I was too young the first time. I was 23. The other guy I met through work and pursued him for a year. When I was giving up, he asked me out but wanted a promise we would be married by 26 and I couldn't promise him that. And [the third] guy was awesome. He treated me with love, taught me how to love and be loved. I didn't know how to do 'love.' I was raised to be the caretaker, so accepting the help back, I didn't feel comfortable with it."

Amber accepts her life, but she is "a constant worrier. I could be better. I feel like I should have sucked it up and married the guy who treated me like gold. If I had learned how to identify what I wanted sooner or [what] would best compliment me, I would have understood he was a great guy . . . he was a 'silent Bob' but a doer, a great listener. He was a great guy, but I needed to come to terms with myself. It was me," My eyes brim with tears for the pain of her self-realization. My compassion overflows and I apologize. She does not want me to feel sorry for her. She has enough self-recrimination for all of midtown Manhattan.

"I had the 'June Cleaver' mentality, the 'Brady Bunch.' I have it in my head that's what I should be, that the man should be more powerful. When I realize in a relationship that I am the stronger person, I have some contempt because I feel the guy should be stronger and I retreat. I want the man to be stronger." *(Oh dear Lord: she's saying she wants the Dude to be the Dude!)*

So what now, Amber? She still dates and has just ended a

year-long relationship with a man with whom she was trying to have a baby.

"We were trying for seven months. The relationship wasn't exactly where I wanted it to be . . . but I thought we would be good together." When there were problems with fertility related to his sperm count, she says he bailed on her. "We were on this path and had an argument. It was stupid and he texted that he couldn't go to the [doctor] appointment. That he needed a break. It really sucked . . . I am older, I don't know what I am going to do now. I think I would be a great mom. I feel bad, but I don't necessarily want to do it on my own."

She is so open and unguarded. She bares her soul in a café on West 57th Street and the rawness of her pain is overwhelming to me. I backpedal from the tears we are both fending off and switch it up a bit. I ask for her thoughts on feminism. Is discrimination something she encounters in her daily life? We both welcome the relief of a more theoretical conversation.

"I started my career in 1995-96 in IT with all these guys," she recalls. "Eventually I became the boss of the department. I hired the best people. Some were women. By time I left that area, it was definitely more mixed. I became the only woman on the leadership side, and now on the business side. I grew up in a corporate career that was all men. It doesn't bother me. It's a fact of life. I also work in a global role and those who don't acknowledge that there is sexism or cultural differences, are fooling themselves. With Chinese and Latin [men], there is a predisposition. They have a different attitude. I don't feel discriminated against, though. It's the way it is. You have to work it the way you can, it's just different."

We invariably head back from the general to the personal.

"This last guy was definitely intimidated by what I do. I made more money than him, had more life experience, had more 'everything' experience, but I thought our emotional connection would trump that. Turns out he was pretty immature . . . but most men are fine with what I do. They . . . diminish it a bit because they don't understand it, especially because it's in fashion. They are more dismissive. But it *is* a business."

On the other hand, she loves "working with strong men. They are more black and white. They have competence, no remorse . . . if they make a mistake, they let it go and move on."

I ask her if, in our striving for equality, we have undervalued men. Not so much undervalued, she says, as needing to find a different way to communicate. "I have to learn a whole new language if I want to have a successful relationship." Amber says that she has to accommodate the less confident men she has begun to date. "Let them feel that they are needed, but not be so needy and dependent. *(I see the Dude puffing out his chest over there across the room.)* I have to get through my day and build a business, but then I have to come home and be more submissive . . . and I love being girly and having a guy be chivalrous, but I have to develop a different persona—the *corporate* persona—in conflict with the *woman* persona."

It is in this part of the conversation that Amber best articulates *my* dilemma-that we have failed to teach our girls that the strong, independent (potent!) woman can live side by side in the same body with the . . . what shall we call it? The *feminine* woman? That doesn't work for me. We don't even have the right language to express that essence that makes a woman different from a man without connoting a fragility or submissive quality. It has been called a softness, a vulnerability, a gentleness but it reads as "less than." And therein lies the problem. We need to develop a good, workable vocabulary for those qualities that make a woman different from a man. But it has to be terminology that doesn't confer a judgment of being less desirable.

"I feel like I am living a double standard," Amber continues. "I don't think women can do it all, but I am not happy with a choice I did not know I was making *(another Amber observation that addresses the universal issue from an individual perspective)*. I desperately wanted kids and I feel sad because I wanted my own genetic mix. I never thought I wouldn't have that. It's sad. I can't go there, because . . ." she takes a big breath and lets out a long, slow sigh. "Because . . . I can't go there. I wish I knew earlier that it doesn't have to be perfect."

It is not a joke. It is real life. Real for so many of our daughters. And no one is laughing.

But wait! 10 months after I meet Amber in that coffee shop, I receive the following email:

Dear Debbie: Exciting news on the relationship front: I am expecting a baby in June!

I almost fall off my chair. Just when I was beginning to reconcile myself to the fact that I might not find a happy ending for this project, Gmail delivers one right to my doorstep . . . I mean laptop. When last we spoke, Amber was nursing the pain of a breakup with the man she thought would father her baby. Had they made up? Had she met someone new?

She writes: In all my forty-something years, I have never been treated so badly by a man and was pretty stunned . . . I would need to go home and cry by 6pm. One night, I was determined to break the pattern and stopped at a swing dance class. I used to dance a lot with this guy and I wanted to "take back my dance" from the memories we shared. When the lesson started, a handsome man came over and asked if I had a partner. We took the class together and he gave me his card. It took me a while to feel more like myself again and to call him. We went out, had lots of chemistry and are still dating. It happened fast, unplanned and he is the dad.

I was quite nervous to tell my family because of my own self-imposed puritanical guilt and it took me a while to reconcile my lifelong responsible behavior versus the one night that has dramatically changed my life. Nonetheless, I finally told my family. They are thrilled . . . Overall, a surprised but very good response.

It's all pretty exciting and a bit daunting!! Despite feelings of fear, I truly feel like this is a miracle baby, a higher plan is at work and it is meant to be. I am thankful for the blessing!

Who says you only get three chances? I can't wait to meet Amber's new daughter!

NINETEEN

A New Bloom

So, *listen*, the kids are pregnant again. They wait to tell me until after the first sonogram. They invite me to the second one. I cry when I see the beating heart of my grandchild. It is miraculous. I understand the lengths a woman will go to conceive and carry a child. It is a gift. It is truly one of the most amazing things on this earth. When it works.

I think we are about twelve weeks along. Finishing the first trimester. I will not celebrate yet. I will not blab to everyone I know. I do tell my college roommate and the book group. The kids want to tell the relatives themselves; this will be the first baby in the next generation of Slevins.

I will hold my breath again. I will not allow myself to love it. I will only anticipate this child in my heart, not out loud. A new baby. The generations turn. We will be the next generation of grandparents (*God willing, I hear my mother-in-law whisper in my head.)*

TWENTY

It's Biology . . . Or It Isn't

Not long ago, my husband came home from work with a flyer about a gender workshop that was being presented by his company. They were hosting Barbara Annis, one of the leading corporate gender specialists in the world, to talk about men and women in the workplace. Over the past 27 years, Annis and her associates have facilitated over 8,000 corporate workshops, leadership assessments and executive coaching sessions. As chair emeritus of the Women's Leadership Board at the Harvard Kennedy School, Annis recently received the International Alliance for Women Lifetime Achievement Award in recognition of her outstanding accomplishments. No slouch, this lady! But what has that got to do with what I am writing about, I asked the hubby.

"I don't know—I think it might be interesting. Come or don't come. Suit yourself. With a whole day of gender stuff, you might find a nugget for your book. Maybe *I* will learn something," he replies. Now I am intrigued.

I get up early and doff my writer duds for some corporate clothing and follow him in my own car so I have a means for escape, should the program prove inexorably boring. Seven hours later, I am the last person to leave the room, smug with the promise that Annis will take my call later in the week. I am firmly gripping her card in my sweaty, opportunistic palm.

Her book *Same Words, Different Language* peeks out from my bag. A coup! Companies pay a fortune for her time and she is willing to give me an hour for free. I love—**LOVE**—what she has to say.

The most fabulous part of the whole day is a power point presentation that shows an MRI of a man's brain and a woman's brain. They are asked by the technician "What are you thinking about?" The man says "Nothing" and his brain study shows very little activity. The woman says "Not much" and her brain is lit up like a Christmas tree with all kinds of cross connections. Annis says that when your man says he is thinking about nothing, he usually is. Women, on the other hand, find it very hard to turn off their thoughts.

Annis has worked with men and women across the globe and I want to know if my topic, this trend toward not coupling, is evident outside the United States.

"It's happening all over the world: Italy, France, Japan," she says. "It comes down to misunderstanding. The sexes are not *communicating*."

So equality is creating greater misunderstanding? More information, please. "Misinterpreting gender differences, this thing about women wanting men to react like they do. We have tolerated the differences," she explains. "In the romantic phase of the relationship, it's great. We are so similar. Then we move into a committed relationship and the romantic stuff goes away and the real man shows up with his differences. Then we try to make them our girlfriends. They are not hardwired this way."

I hear the echoes of Dr. Landsman: "It's biology, baby." Have we come so far only to find that we are back at the beginning? Biological organisms with innate differences predetermined to mate in a specific way. When (if ever,) I scream inside my head, does intellectual choice override biological drive?

She talks about the large swath of women who divorce in middle age. "It boils down to a serious lack of understanding of the differences between men and women. We think it's fixable. Again, it is hardwired. Women enter the relationship based on his potential—they will 'work' on him. And that's the last thing men want." There it is again: biology.

"Men come into a relationship hoping a woman will never change. Woman exit saying 'I tried everything.' Men exit saying, 'I don't know this woman anymore. She changed.' We don't have a fundamental understanding of each other. The Women's Movement wasn't wrong. It had noble and passionate intentions but the downside of it was that it *suppressed* differences. 'Anything you can do, I can do better.' Gender equality meant treating people the same. But it had some blind spots," Annis says. "The research wasn't there. We didn't have MRI and PET scanners to look at live tissue. We only looked at nurture not nature. Now we can't deny it. It was a big 'aha moment.'"

In *Same Words, Different Language*, she writes:

> Technology and sophisticated research techniques allowed scientists to observe actual differences in the ways men and women's brains work . . . men's brains were on average, up to 10% larger than women's . . . women's brains contained more nerve cells and had significantly more connections for neuron firings, which are messages sent between various parts of the brain. In women's brains, for instance, the part of the brain associated with language skills contained up to 11% more brain cells than the corresponding part in men's brains.[1]

(Hah! I knew it! I guess that is why I often feel like I am talking to myself when I am talking to my husband. Too many brain cells for balanced conversation. Since Annis says it is biology, I guess I should just get over it.)

"This was just the beginning," Annis writes. "Throughout the 1980s and 1990s scientists came to discover that men and women actually thought and processed information differently."

She goes on to list many differences that became evident in the laboratory such as:

> Women are stronger in verbal fluency.
> Men are stronger in spatial relations.
> Women can remember lists of words better.
> Men can mentally rotate images.
> Men are better at orienting themselves in a closed space and navigating themselves through a route.
> Women are better at recalling the landmarks along that same route.

I could continue, but you get the point. Annis says:

> Differences between men and women are in part the result of evolution . . . virtually every professional scientist and researcher who works in the field of gender has concluded that men's and women's brains are different and those differences influence everything we do.[2]

Psychiatrist Rosalind Barnett and media critic Caryl Rivers don't necessarily agree. In their 2004 book *Same Difference*, they contend that:

> Rigid norms, not biology, are operating here. As gender

> roles loosen . . . women's and men's behavior reflect many forces: their gender, their individual talents and preferences, their personalities and the situations they find themselves in.[3]

The women acknowledge gender differences but argue that, "the part they play in our lives is far less important than most people assume." They write that the *assumption* of these differences actually plays more havoc with gender relations than the differences themselves, particularly with regard to education, division of labor in the work place and at home.

> If we believe that men and women are innately different . . . we won't expand parental leave for fathers . . . because [they] are not natural caregivers . . . we will set up separate educational facilities for boys and girls and teach all girls one way and all boys another, so lots of kids won't get the teaching that's right for them. We'll create suspicion between men and women."[4]

I wanted to believe that the difference between Annis' position and the position of Barnett and Rivers is a function of research and information garnered during the years between each book's publication. Unfortunately, that is not the case. Annis first published in 2003 and reissued her book in 2010. Barnett and Rivers published in 2004. A year apart and such different conclusions; it doesn't help me much.

Same Difference takes the argument about gender differentiation back to early childhood saying that many children at a young age tend to prefer toys designed for their sex. "Are such preferences due to deep seated, inborn differences, as many experts and laypeople have assumed?" they ask. "Or can they be traced back to early stereotyping?"[5]

The National Association for Single Sex Education has a lot to say about this, specifically with regard to schooling.[6] In addition to citing a cross cultural report by the National Institute of Health that supports these differences across a significant number of European, African and Asian countries, they include on their website a study by Eva Pomerantz, Ellen Altermatt, & Jill Saxon,[7] which says:

> Girls generalize the meaning of their failures because they interpret them as indicating that they have disappointed adults, and thus they are of little worth. Boys, in contrast, appear to see their failures as relevant only to the specific subject area in which they have failed; this may be due to their relative lack of concern with pleasing adults. In addition, because girls view evaluative feedback as diagnostic of their abilities, failure may lead them to incorporate this information into their more general view of themselves.

One of the most compelling arguments for me on gender differences is actually made by Canadian-American blogger and modern day feminist, Anita Sarkeesian. I was turned onto her by one of the women I profiled, Christiane, who said that I must include her in any discussion of the differences between the sexes. Although she has received some negative backlash and been involved with some controversies, she adds tremendous value to feminist dialogues. Sarkeesian produces the video blog (or vlog) Feminist Frequency that skewers the toy and gaming industry for creating sex-specific toys and games. She does such a number on Legos, and their misguided attempt to create sex-specific *building blocks. (REALLY!? Building blocks?)* I thought I should apologize to my children of both sexes and give away the two crates of "boy-colored" Legos in the garage that are awaiting

If you aren't familiar with Sarkeesian, take five minutes and check her out. You will be glad you did. With a scientist's mind, a researcher's dedication and a hipster's style, she presents a passionate case for the way girls are manipulated through playthings to view the world in a certain way. She has turned the toy industry upside down for me. I will confide that she is the only person who did not answer my repeated requests for an interview, but I respect her work so much and understand her reticence (she has received death threats for her position) that I am including her anyway.

It's also appropriate to weigh in here with Peggy Orenstein's book *Cinderella Ate My Daughter*. She nails the predicament in her very first chapter "Why I Hoped for a Boy":

> Princesses are just a phase, after all. It's not as though girls are still swanning about in their Sleeping Beauty gowns when they leave for college . . . but they did mark my daughter's first foray into the mainstream culture, the first time the influences extended beyond the family. And what was the first thing the culture told her about being a girl? Not that she was competent, strong, creative or smart, but what every little girl wants—or should want—to be the Fairest Of Them All.[And live Happily Ever After] The more mainstream media girls

consume," she writes, "the more importance they place on being pretty and sexy.[8]

When Orenstein is done with princesses she goes on to pink. The color not the singer (Pink the singer is actually a great example of a strong independent woman). "It's not intrinsically bad, but it is such a tiny slice of the rainbow."[9] This is where Sarkeesian shines. She cites the embracing of pink as a major marketing strategy of Legos for girls. There are kits to build homes and beauty parlors—all very pink and lavender—where the boys are given airports and construction vehicles. In khaki.

"One of the easiest ways to segment a market is to magnify gender differences—or invent them where they did not previously exist," writes Orenstein.[10] She points out that all female versions of board games appear to have been dipped in Pepto Bismol. "The innocence that pink signaled during the Princess years, which seemed so benign, even protective, has receded, leaving behind narcissism and materialism as hallmarks of feminine identity."[11]

I am torn by this discussion. Having had a girl first, followed by two boys, my field experience supports a strong innate gender preference. Trying to live up to the image of the non-sexist parent I thought myself to be, I offered my children gender-neutral clothing and toys very early on. Unfortunately, they were not onboard with my political leanings. They were *very* specific about what was "girl's" or "boy's" clothing and showed a marked preference with their toys.

Take Barbie, for instance. I gave my daughter trucks as well as Barbie dolls. She used the trucks to chauffer the Barbies across her room to tea parties. The boys, on the other hand, took the old Barbies and tied them up or ran over them with their trucks in simulated war games. Occasionally, a mummified doll with its overly-sexualized body fully obscured by duct tape, would be propelled through the sky as a human bomb. Same toys, different interpretations. If they were socialized to those behaviors, it came from outside our home or from the limited and carefully screened media that came into the house. I swear it wasn't *me*! I tried so hard!

As Orenstein attacks the marketing of a femininity that was determined by some research and development focus group she touches on an issue that has been paramount for many of the men I interviewed. Weight. And I HATE this—wait—let me repeat I really HATE this (although I am so glad she says it).

Orenstein asserts:

> Regardless of what we say, from the get-go everything, everyone else, in our culture tells girls that their weight and looks matter—a lot. Though appearance shouldn't dictate how they are treated by others—let alone their self-worth—it does. Talent? Effort? Intelligence? All are wonderful, yet by middle school, how a girl feels about her appearance—particularly whether she is thin enough, pretty enough and hot enough—has become the single most important determinant of her self-esteem.[12]

Thank you for this, Barbie.

So where does that leave women like Lila, Melanie, and my daughter? They are all beauties. All women who have the talent, have put in the effort, possess the intelligence and *have* embraced the standard of beauty imposed on them by our culture. The triple and quadruple threats. And still. Still. STILL. They cannot find a husband.

Peggy Orenstein hears me and the rest of the mothers of the legions of the unmarried:

> I may want my girl to do and be whatever she dreams of as an adult, but I also hope she will find her Prince (or Princess) Charming and make me a grandma. I do not want her to be a fish without a bicycle; I want her to be a fish with another fish. Preferable a fish who loves and respects her and also does dishes, his share of the laundry and half the child care.[13]

I am supremely confused now. Is it biology? Is it marketing? Is it acculturation? With a deep respect for science and what you can see on an MRI, I tend to lean towards Annis' concrete representation of our innate differences. But as a believer in all things empirical and an observant parent, our culture has done much to perpetuate stereotypic sex roles.

"I really think that we need to look at it in an inclusive way," Annis tells me. "The Women's Movement became inclusive: learning, gender differences. If we want to know how to have a brilliant relationship and marriage, we have to move forward and not base it on past experiences . . . it's important to see that it is possible to have non-traditional, co-collaborating relationships." Science aside.

"It's really, really simple," Annis says. "You don't have to boil the ocean. We didn't know what we didn't know." Okay.

So now we know. We are wired differently. The Dude wants to be the Dude. A young woman doesn't need to be a Disney Princess. What do we do with that information? How do our young women use it to find and forge lasting relationships that might pave the way to the families they want?

Hellllooooo? I am not hearing an answer, only a description of a problem that has been defined for me over and over. Dr. Nachtigall says it is a numbers game. She has cared for thousands of women in her many years of practice. And she advises them all: go. Get out there. Start your engines, ladies. The future awaits.

***

I have saved Sarah for last because her story tells the story of this generation. She is a 35-year-old businesswoman who has crafted her own outstanding success. A graduate of a very prestigious business school, she lives in Silicon Valley where she created her own software company and recently sold it for a large profit. She is busy traveling and contemplating what is next.

"This is a story that hasn't been told," she says of my study. She is able to separate the personal from the global. "It is fascinating—I don't think anybody understands what is going on. There is the meta level—what's happening culture wide. I would never have predicted it would be so complicated . . . [and] I never imagined I would be 35 and not married. I never thought it *wouldn't* happen. That's just something that happens to people. They fall in love and it happens. [It is an] interesting and challenging time . . . I read articles about Millennials. The values they have are part of the change we are all experiencing, [they are] getting it from stories that have been written by our generation. When I was 15, I never thought it would be like this. I feel like it happened *to* me; I don't feel like I set out to be a career women and then changed my mind."

The daughter of a "really messy divorce" Sarah says, "I was traumatized by that. My generation—we have seen portrayals of marriage in media that are complex and negative . . . [I had] 20 years of indoctrination of what can go wrong in relationships."

Sarah sees connections where others might shrug and move on. She is a child of popular culture. "The rom-coms *[romantic comedies]* are dying out. The cultural sensibilities have changed. We live in a hook-up culture. It's hard to find romance. I am financially and professionally standing on my own two feet, but chivalry is still not dead in my generation. I am looking for a man who is a little stronger to lean on. I don't want to be dominated, but want the classic male/female dynamic." *Is she looking for The Dude?*

I ask her what messages she got from her parents about marriage and family, aside from the inadvertent ones. "My parents always wanted me to fully express [myself] as a person . . . they hoped that would include finding a partner and having a family. As I got older and had experiences with men who weren't good for me, my dad did say 'better off on your own than racing from man to man.' My mother wants me to meet someone and have a family. If I had a daughter now, I would want her to meet a wonderful man who would support her, and build a family together."

Sarah says she doesn't "like to think about how hard it is.

There are so many forces making this difficult . . . if I had ever been just focused on career, maybe I would look at myself differently. I did that for short periods of time in life, but I had a long relationship from 16-26. When it ended, I was devastated. Had I stayed with him, it would not have precluded having a family . . . when it ended I focused full-time on my career, from 27-30. I had relationships, but it was harder."

I want to know if her success intimidates the men she meets, as she is not at all a corporate type and upon meeting her you might underestimate her business prowess. She is petite, pretty and a bit bohemian. She is also *wicked* smart, as they say in Boston, and that becomes apparent from a first introduction.

"People always think I intimidate men, but I don't think so. I do way more listening than talking . . . the hard part is finding someone who would be a good partner for me. I keep the list really simple: trust and feel safe with, attracted to each other, would make a good father." Seems reasonable to me.

Has that guy ever turned up? "I have shed enough tears to fertilize a desert over this," Sarah says. "I met this person when I was very young. It doesn't mean I will never find it again." She continues to scour the market.

"I think I have done everything most women have done. I stopped counting at 110 first dates over a three-year period, because it was such an obscene number it was ridiculous. I went to counseling to talk about this. What's holding me back? I did everything I could think to do—explored everything."

Sarah says she was just exhausted. "I wasn't meeting men that I was drawn to. And those that I did have a relationship with, there was some kind of fatal flaw that made it not work. Was I being too picky? Was it worth staying in the relationship even though I was hurting? I was dating a guy who said he would never want kids—that's a deal breaker. This stuff is hard: trying to find a partner that you feel good with, feel safe, have an attraction . . . [there are] so many things to line up . . . we see divorce as more likely. I don't want to put my kids through that. We have to look at it more carefully. In past generations, there were fewer professional women, so the bar for men now is higher since women are more professional. [And if] a woman is the primary breadwinner, having kids, that is really, really hard. Men aren't moving into the caretaker role with the same enthusiasm as women are moving into professional roles."

Sarah illuminates an interesting point. Women have made huge gains in what has been predominantly male territory, but the guys are not banging down the door to stay home and keep house. Seriously, can you blame them? There is a reason the Women's Movement started in the first place and I am sure it had as much to do with the drudgery of laundry and cleaning the providing of maid service for a family—as it did the search for intellectual fulfillment.

"We are coming to the end of a certain era," she says, "but adjustments haven't been made. I am meeting guys 38-40 who still aren't ready. If I date a guy my age, he probably isn't thinking like I am thinking. He still thinks about playing around, and when they *are* ready, these men are looking for women who are 30 because they have 'a lot more runway.'" OMG! What an expression. It resonates for days and I repeat it many times. Why does it bother me so? I think it is because it provokes an image of a woman as something to be rolled over, utilized for take-off or a safe landing, although Sarah does not mean it in that way. But it smacks of skid marks, nevertheless.

There is such sadness and resignation in Sarah's voice as we speak. "I feel like I have given up. That's very recent for me. At this moment, it's extremely demoralizing for anyone to continue to put energy into something that isn't getting anywhere. We want to put our energy into things that will make us happy, or others happy, that will bear fruit. I know women who are doing everything they can to put themselves out there. You do a lot of work on yourself, find and eliminate your blindspot. You do all this work and it doesn't happen and doesn't happen. You are banging your head against a wall. I need to find what else I can make my life about."

She tells me that she is doing a lot of soul searching right now. "I thought I would have a family, and this is something that can't be controlled. I don't know what it looks like yet, not 100% sure how to design it, but what does my life look like if I live it alone . . . I have looked into egg freezing, but I have never wanted to have a baby no matter what. I always thought it would come out of a relationship. I think about it, but I am not quite there yet. It's *hard* to think about. I feel very much alone all the time . . . when you go this long without a partner and you do everything by yourself, it's a lonely place."

The thing that intrigues me most about Sarah is that regardless of her own personal situation, she still sees the greater picture. She understands she is part of a larger phenomenon.

"There have been decades of media about unhappy marriages. [There is] a huge trend of people thinking that marriage won't make them happy anymore. I meet lots of men who say that. The roles have changed so much that they don't know which end is up . . . there is no longer a stigma around divorce. If you are unhappy, you split. Women don't have the option of not paying attention to their careers. A lot of women choose their careers because they can't depend on their marriages being there."

She drives the nail in with a mighty hammer. This *is* what we have wrought. We have helped out daughters get out of the house and into the universities, the workplace, the *professions*. They pay their own rent or purchase their own homes. They buy cashmere and cars. They travel. They invest in and for themselves and have careers managing money for others. Competent. Independent. They have learned to be afraid of *not* being self-supporting. And the men have taken their cues from this rhetoric. "What do they need *me* for, they ask. What role can I serve?" Just how does The Dude deliver for women stuck in the unpregnant pause?

TWENTY-ONE

Hip To Be Single

You know something is changing when *The New York Times* does a huge feature article on it. When it's on the front of the Sunday travel section. And two weeks later, the real estate section. NEWS FLASH: It's suddenly hip to be single. Is it because the writers of those articles are of that generation or at least have their finger on the pulse of it enough to spin the conversation to find the glass half full? Are they trying to justify their own choices? Or is it that the tide is really turning? I hope it is the tide.

Although the statistics offer evidence of more singles, they don't necessarily indicate the state of satisfaction with that state. But big splashy articles in the *Times* do *(kind of)*. At least to the population I have been interviewing.

Picture this: A tropical setting. You are poolside with a Skinny Girl margarita. The sun is just beginning its descent toward the horizon, streaking the sky with the same hot pink and fuchsia that adorns your Tory Burch sandals. Your iPad mini has been stocked with three industry insider books and one well-recommended novel. You close your eyes and let the last of the day's warmth caress your body. You don't have to move. You are free to stay there until the pool boy rolls away your chaise. No one is expecting you anywhere. No deadlines and no demands. You are experiencing The Westin Grand

Central Hotel's "Womanhood Redefined" package. According to *Times* writer Stephanie Rosenbloom, it includes a consultation about healthful eating habits with the hotel's executive chef, a 30-minute meeting with the hotel's running expert, a $25 food and drink credit, a 10% discount on yoga classes, a Westin white tea candle and a new book, *Otherhood: Modern Women Finding a New Kind of Happiness* by Melanie Notkin.

Rosenbloom zeroes in on why the Westin trip is different from a "girls' getaway weekend" and how it ties into the book. "The definition of an "Otherhood" woman in the book is one who, like the author, wants to be in love and married with children," she writes. "She is single, 'long past the time when she thought she'd be settled down,' as opposed to the woman who actively chooses not to have children—or a husband or wife, for that matter."[1] These are the women suspended in the unpregnant pause. And they need a vacation. A vacation from everyone asking them "are you seeing anyone?" as if that is the major measure of their worth.

With almost half the population of women in the fertile/ marrying bracket *not* getting married, you have to ask yourself how long until smart marketers are all over this demographic. Not long, obviously. Westin is all over it. They have it covered.

"In 1949, the Yale anthropologist George Peter Murdock published a survey of some "representative cultures" from . . . diverse parts of the world," writes Eric Klinenberg in his book *Going Solo*. "He reported, 'The nuclear family is a universal human social grouping . . . it exists as a distinct and strongly functional group in every known society.'"

But not anymore, Klinenberg says:

> Today, more than 50% of American adults are single, and 31 million—roughly one out of every seven adults—live alone . . . contemporary solo dwellers are primarily women: about 17 million compared to 14 million men. The majority, more than 15 million, are between the ages of thirty-five and sixty-four . . . unlike their predecessors, people who live alone today cluster together in metropolitan areas and inhabit all regions of the country.[2]

And lest you think that Americans are alone in being alone, "the four countries with the highest rates of living alone are Sweden, Norway, Finland and Denmark, where roughly 40 to 45% of all households have just one person," Klinenberg reports.

Like many of the professionals I have spoken with, Klinenberg focuses on the culture of choice:

> The search for success and happiness depends less on tying oneself down to another than on opening up the world of possibilities . . . freedom. Flexibility. Personal choice. These rank among our most cherished modern virtues.

> Not long ago, someone who was dissatisfied with his or her spouse and wanted a divorce had to justify that decision. Today . . . if you are not fulfilled with your marriage, you have to justify staying in it, because of the tremendous cultural pressure to be good to one's self.[3]

This speaks to Father Jim's observation about personal fulfillment being the overriding goal of this generation and my interviews back it up. Almost all the women I spoke with emphasized that they were raised with the mantra, "do what makes you happy." Unfortunately, putting oneself first and making oneself happy is not high on the list of successful parenting skills. Self-fulfillment almost always takes a back seat to a sick baby.

So, here we go again: let's blame it on the Women's Movement. Klinenberg writes with no malice[4]:

> Begin with the rising status of women, whose advances range from gains in education and massive incorporation into the paid labor force to the right to control their domestic, sexual and reproductive lives . . . women's assertion of control over their own bodies has also changed the terms of modern relationships, resulting in delayed marriage, a longer transition to adulthood, and increased rates of separation and divorce.
>
> The second driving force, behind the cult of the individual is the communications revolution, which has allowed people throughout the world to experience the pleasures of social life—not to mention vast amounts of entertainment—even when they're home alone.

Much of Klinenberg's information comes from a seven-year study he did that began with Manhattan, which he calls "the nation's most popular place for living alone."[5] It eventually expanded to other major American cities including Los

Angeles, Chicago, Washington, DC, Austin and the San Francisco Bay Area.

He asks some probing questions along the way. "Does the rise of living alone stem from . . . a growing sense of distrust—of others, of intimate relationships?" and "Does living alone mean something different now that we're hyperconnected, through cell phones, social media, and the like?" while wondering about "singles in their thirties and forties who refuse to compromise in their search for a partner, in no small part because they recognize and enjoy the benefits (personal, social, and sexual) of living alone." So do I. And there's that word again: compromise.

"They stay in school longer," he writes. "They delay marriage and having children and spend years engaging in casual sex or serial dating, often remaining skeptical that an intimate relationship can last a lifetime."[6] My point exactly. And just how, may I ask, did they develop that attitude about intimate relationships? *Oh wait!* Let's look again at the divorce rates. Bingo.

But Klinenberg doesn't see this delay as a negative. He says the young singletons he interviewed "actively reframe living alone as a mark of distinction and success, not social failure. They use it as a way to invest time in their personal growth and, above all, professional growth." He says they make "great efforts to be social: building up a strong network of friends and work contacts . . . that substitute for families by providing community and support."[7]

And they feel good about their lives. He directs his reader to the Los Angeles-based SingularCity.com, a website for all things single. Just a cursory glance can make you feel left out if you are married and not having all the great experiences highlighted in this online magazine.

But there are drawbacks to the single life, as Klinenberg points out midway through his book. Like getting sick. Or aging alone. It is important to develop a network. Which brings me to the **other** *New York Times* hot topic article: *The Buddy System*. "For some New Yorkers," reads the caption beneath several attractive groupings of people, "sharing an apartment with others is a choice, not a necessity. The list of advantages starts with built-in companionship."[8]

Reporter Joanne Kaufman lays out the case for communal living. In addition to easing the financial burden of maintaining a city apartment by yourself and freeing a portion of income for other pursuits, she writes that "roommates provide a built-in social network and act as a resident sounding board, career counselor, dinner companion, love doctor and hedge against loneliness."[9]

Like the decrease in marriages and the decline of the birth rate, living alone is a fairly new phenomenon. Klinenberg writes that our species has about 200,000 years of collective living experience "and only about fifty or sixty years with our experiment in going solo on a massive scale . . . we've yet to develop any serious public responses to the challenges of living alone."[10]

He mentions the lack of "affordable housing for younger and middle-aged singletons . . . metropolitan areas weren't built for them and we've failed to redesign cities and suburbs to meet the needs of a singleton society."[11] He stresses the need for walkable neighborhoods with proximity to a "range of commercial goods and services, attractive public spaces, and restaurants, bars, and cafes where residents can meet . . . they are especially important for those who live alone, because they are such heavy users of the places that support local social life."[12] Hence, Manhattan.

Like every other person I spoke to regarding this book, Klinenberg found that American women in their late thirties and early forties consistently reported that their anxieties around reproduction cause them to doubt if they made good decisions about their personal and professional lives. "They tear themselves up asking questions that few American men who live alone ponder: should they have settled, or settled down, earlier? Would they have been happier if they had lowered their professional ambitions and invested more time in their personal lives?"[13]

It is interesting to note that although the Swedish women in his study did share some of those anxieties, they felt less of a push to find the right partner because of the generous state and employer support available for childcare, where "no family can pay more than 1 to 3 percent of their income; and public health care ranks among the finest in the world."[14]

I am thinking it's time for action, a new coalition born from the frustration of missing the boat. A call for progressive legislation that provides better maternal/child health care and child care so that anyone who wants a child can have one.

The women entering the unpregnant pause have the talent and maybe even the time. Can you imagine what all that untapped estrogen might produce? If they are not making babies, at least let them make change.

TWENTY-TWO

What's Next?

So: retirement. Who's ready for retirement and what has that got to do with our daughters stuck in the unpregnant pause? Everything.

I thought I would raise my kids, work part-time and go full-time into the workforce when the youngest left the nest. Put in a few good years, make a little money then retire and help with the grandkids. And I have done that, except for the grandkids.

I am finally building the career that I didn't have time or inclination for in my twenties and early thirties. I didn't understand then what moved and motivated me, what I could immerse myself in deeply enough to lose track of time and work late into the night. I wanted to love something so much that I would forget to eat *(just kidding—no matter how great the project, I never forget to eat)*. At that time, I couldn't imagine doing something so fulfilling that the idea of retirement would lose its appeal. I thought I would just walk away—from whatever it *was* I was doing—and help my children with *their* children. Now I want both. It's not all that different from the choices mothers are asked to make, except that a grandma goes home to quiet at the end of the day.

I share with Dr. Diller, one of the esteemed psychologists I have consulted, that I am exploring the question of grandparenthood. She surprises me by saying that in her practice, a narrow sliver of New York City population that lives in the rarified air around Park Avenue, the women are not at all concerned with becoming grandparents. Her clients are in Africa on safari, or in India at an ashram, in Thailand hanging with the elephants. Or working. They don't have *time* for grandchildren. With extended life expectancy and fortunate financial status, they are cramming every possible experience that their health and physical abilities allow into the remaining years. They are not alone. In increasing numbers, Americans all across the country are delaying retirement. The U.S. Census Bureau provides the following statistics in an article entitled "Labor Force Projections to 2014: Retiring Boomers."

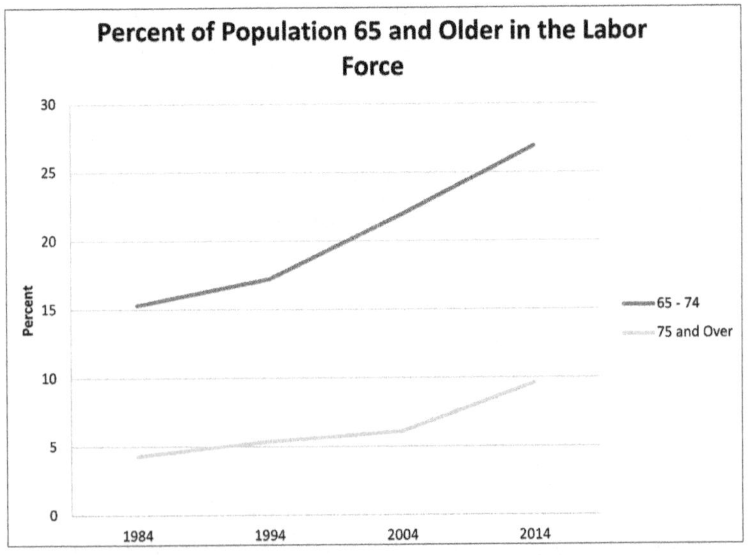

I too, would like to continue to work and have the opportunity to travel and explore all the things I didn't have time or funds for when my children were young. But what about legacy? That matters to me also. Who will remember that I made delicious chocolate chip cookies or the best latkes? That my arms were always open and my ears ready to listen? My travel agent? Certainly no one will care how many hours I logged at work, other than to resent it on a different therapist's couch somewhere down the road.

Some may ask if it's important to be remembered for my cookies. And it probably isn't. (Yes. Yes, it is.) But for all the negative memories I have from growing up, I do remember my mother's sour cream coffee cake. I remember how the kitchen smelled: warm and sweet with the intermingled aroma of chocolate and cinnamon . . . sprinkled with camaraderie. I remember her happy at those times. Laughing. Mixing. Making a big mess in the kitchen. I remember leaning into the Formica counter and breaking off a bit of caramelized crust from the bottom of the cake, basking in my mother's giddy joy of creating, of eating what she baked. For an hour, she wasn't angry or resentful or depressed. I remember *me* happy. Isn't that important? (Yes. It. Is.)

I want to make those memories for my future grandchildren, in-between seeing more of this vast world. But what if there are no grandchildren? How will I redefine what retirement looks like?

Before I lean into my walker or have to buy one of those nifty motorized scooters, there is still time to do interesting things. There are projects and trips and new stuff to learn. Classes and elder hostels. New movies and old books waiting to be read or reread. Lots to *do*, but none of these activities fill the longing in my heart for new life—a new generation. The future.

That yearning pushes me into another conundrum: the "Doggie Dilemma." Should I get a dog? Should I *not* get a dog?

If I don't have any grandbabies, a dog can fill that specific need to nurture. They are cuddly/cute/good companionship. I can take the dog to PetSmart and buy her a toy. I can knit a sweater for the dog. She can stay home by herself, but will be so grateful if I take her with me for a walk/in the car/in the bike basket. She will warm my feet on cold nights and she will love me unconditionally. She will even lick my face, which is more than I can say for a grandchild *or husband* for that matter. I can even bake her doggie biscuits. Being the dog of a non-grandma is a pretty big responsibility. (Update: *I got the dog. She's a spoiled bitch.*)

If you are not into the doggie scene, there is always volunteerism. The world is filled with a million needy causes. With a little computer know-how, a willing and giving soul can pair with a myriad of organizations that would be grateful for the help and skill set. Because I have a profound need for deep emotional connection, I have become an end-of-life doula. That means that I am part of a team that ministers to the dying so that no one dies alone and no family member is alone with the dying, unless they choose to be. I believe deeply, in my heart of hearts, that as we welcome a new life into this world, so should we help an old one exit. We run to the hospital with arms outstretched to receive a new baby. Can we not hold the hand of our dying loved ones as they slip back from where they came? "I wouldn't be able to do it," friends say. That's okay. It's not for everyone, I do it because I can.

If end-of-life care is not for you, hold babies in foster care. Photograph rescue animals for adoption websites. Do accounting/publicity/marketing for an important cause. Bake cookies for a bake sale. Or sell cookies and start a new business. Retirement without grandchildren can be a full and rewarding experience. I know that. It's just not the experience *I* want.

All baking aside, there is much to consider as we move forward in our lives with daughters (and sons) who do not marry. As we age, ourselves *and* our children, new concerns arise. The biggest issue for me is that of the "Significant Other," the name that goes in the box on every form we fill out in daily life: emergency contact.

If there is no spouse: who ya gonna call? And lest you think I am implying our daughters don't have wonderful friends to take them to medical procedures, help them move, pick them up if they drink too much or break an ankle at the gym—they do. I am actually talking about *my* generation. You all know this to be true that unless we are near death, if our daughters need us, we will get to them in whatever way we can. We are mothers, First and Foremost. But our daughters are our daughters, and although they may love us and drop what they are doing to help us, very often we are *their* support. And even more often, we don't want to burden them.

So what does this mean going forward? I am afraid to say. I see single daughters managing their mothers' illnesses, driving to daily radiation appointments, cooking meals, taking care of elderly fathers, arranging for aids and then assisted living facilities. At the end of their day they go home alone. Who will rub their feet, bring a glass of wine or cup of coffee, or hold them when the fear of losing their mother or father, *their* significant other, becomes too much to bear? The dog? Having no one to share the emotional burden of an aging parent is a great sadness in itself. Yes, there *are* sons. And sons can be doting, but as many of the staff will tell you in late-in-life care facilities, it is usually the daughter who bears the brunt of the aging parent.

If you want to buy your daughters a gift, even the married ones, buy yourself a long-term care insurance policy. They will thank you every day of your eventual decline. Lucky for me, my husband insisted my mother buy a policy while she was still working. It was my saving grace during her three-year decline from Alzheimer's disease. It offered me the option between excellent care and . . . who knows what. I can't even imagine the alternative. A crappy facility? Moving in with me? We have already established that I didn't even *like* my mother very much, so I certainly wasn't bringing her into my home to nurse her through her final years of insanity.

In the book *The Age of Aging* by George Magnus the author depicts how family life has changed over the last 100 years:

> Childless couples and single-parent families comprise a growing social class, and care for separated and single middle-aged women, as they age, becomes a more pressing issue when they do not have adult children to help.[1]

Not only will they have the burden of caring for *us*, but who will take care of them?

What will old age look like for a generation with fewer children? Who will hold up the enormous debt of social security? As the fertility rate goes down, there will be less workers to support the aging population. There will be a decline in child-dependency and an increase in old-age dependency. Old-age dependency, Magnus says, is much more costly:

> Birth rates have fallen well below the replacement rate

> of the population in many rich and some poor countries at a time when the age structure is shifting steadily toward older groups. With that comes the threat of economic decline and rising social tension.[2]

Let me say it again: long term health care insurance.. Not just for you, but for your daughter. Buy it now, for both of you. Then sit back and relax. You're covered.

I have many questions and very few answers for what the future holds. I don't have a crystal ball, but I am alarmed and afraid. Mine may not be the "Greatest Generation," but we are a pretty good one. As is the next. Still, I worry about their future.

Dr. Diller offers up some consolation:

> Remember, life expectancy has risen from age 48 to 78 in a relatively short period of time, which means for the first time in history there are now decades between middle age and the end of life. Many of us thought we would retire by 65, but can't. And those who are fortunate to have that option often choose to work. Even if we're comfortably retired, we want to remain vital and healthy enough to enjoy the years we have left—and that takes effort, time and money. Bottom line, if we choose to help out with grandkids, we expect that they will fit into our busy lives—not the other way around.[3]

I hope I at least have the option.

TWENTY-THREE

It's Technology, Baby

I am over the moon. I am about to meet Dr. Arthur Caplan. Dr. Caplan is a world-renowned thinker on Bioethics. The author of 32 books, he is the founding director of the Division of Medical Ethics at NYU Langone Medical Center's Department of Population Health. Prior to coming to NYU, Caplan created the Center for Bioethics and the Department of Medical Ethics at the University of Pennsylvania Perelman School of Medicine.

He has also served on numerous national and international committees including: the Chair, National Cancer Institute Biobanking Ethics Working Group; the Chair of the Advisory Committee to the United Nations on Human Cloning; the Chair of the Advisory Committee to the Department of Health and Human Services on Blood Safety and Availability; a member of the Presidential Advisory Committee on Gulf War Illnesses; the special advisory committee to the International Olympic Committee on genetics and gene therapy; the ethics committee of the American Society of Gene Therapy; the special advisory panel to the National Institutes of Mental Health on human experimentation on vulnerable subjects and the Wellcome Trust on research in humanitarian crises. He is currently the ethics advisor on synthetic biology to the Defense *Advanced Research Projects Agency*, an agency of the United States Department of Defense.

I *know*. It goes on and on. I am not trying to impress you by providing this partial listing of his credits and accomplishments; I want to make the point that he is *the voice* of our time on bioethics. He practically invented the subject. I have read his commentaries in the paper and seen him on television. I think he has just about the coolest job I can imagine. He is charged with *thinking* about the implications of modern medicine and the future of the human race. A pretty grand assignment, no? Just thinking about *that* makes my brain hurt, so to have an hour of his time is a gift indeed.

I don't know what I was expecting (maybe a stern professor?) but I am taken aback by the enthusiastic guy with the shock of white hair who comes out of his office to greet me with an extended hand. He has a wide, easy smile and such an inviting manner that I am relaxed in no time. I am on the clock, so I get right down to it.

My opening salvo: what does the future look like for women who delay childbearing to pursue careers?

"The more women delay childbearing, the more they use infertility services to help them. That is just a small part of what the future holds. I think the future holds using the techniques . . . to make children with traits that you want for the fertile. The future of infertility treatment is *not* infertility. It is *making* babies. I don't know how fast it's going to come, but you can see it already . . . you see inroads beginning, having to do with eugenics not infertility."

The next thing he says is both illuminating and disturbing. "The market is not big enough to handle all the practitioners," he says of the fertility doctors. "They have to create demand by building a market."

Is this a *commercial* enterprise, I ask. He tells me women use fertility services for all kinds of reasons, one of which is to have a "rescue baby." I have not heard this term before and he explains that when a couple has a seriously sick child, they may look to have another child that might be a possible bone marrow donor. One sibling rescues another with its genetic material.

"Biological life insurance has got a future . . . but the big market is in designer babies, not in biological life insurance—that's a niche. I think we will get into a very different set of debates ethically. Now we talk about abortion. Tomorrow, when someone wants a baby, can they have one without doing genetic testing and design? If you get rid of Roe vs. Wade, you may be opening the door to a very unexpected future where the government can say the 'only acceptable way to have a baby is to have one with certain genetic traits and we are going to impose that on you.'"

My mind is racing with the implications. A genetically predetermined population? A Perfect(ed) Race? But wait! I can see the possibilities. Maybe we can eliminate color-blindness from my family line. My son, my brother, my uncle, my great-uncle: all limited to a narrow palette of the world's glorious colors. Fix it with gene manipulation? Boom. Done.

Caplan takes this discussion further down the road to the future while veering back to the marketplace. "If you really get into healthcare costs, the only way to contain that is to make healthier people. I am not saying that will happen, but it opens the door to that. Once you let the government into your womb, it opens that door. One moral question is this: should people be free to reproduce or not . . . to make better babies or not? We would have to accept people who would have babies with disease."

He explains to me that this is already happening. "Peer pressure and cultural norms create designer babies. The elimination of Down syndrome is a cultural pressure. Look around," he says. "You don't see it anymore . . . commercial forces can drive this. In Singapore, everyone wants smarter babies. That's how they make their living. It's a city-state that depends on smarts. The pressure would be there to have smarter babies. They would do it. Any country that has people competing to get their kids into kindergarten would have a set of people who would do it pretty fast." He repeats it for emphasis lest I not understand the implications for upscale New Yorkers. "Pretty fast!" he says with a chuckle and a shake of his snowy head.

And again, we are back to the marketplace. "The 'one percent' want to stay the 'one percent.' Not only would they want to do it, they would feel they have a duty to do that. They have spent their whole lives working to have money . . . [they would] feel an *obligation* to do it . . . add it up: business opportunity, changing technology, a demand to put to use capacity, a culture that values certain traits, competitiveness. You've got a stew that will produce better babies. To me it's just *when*, not *if*." **YIKES**. It's a scary road ahead.

As technology has the ability to screen for disease, Caplan says it is a short jump to the debate about what are diseases and what are disorders that are just disliked. "Tall, freckled, musical aptitude, keen vision, better memory—that would be hard to argue against. Eliminate homosexuality? Would most people remove it? Sure, people like themselves. They tend to want to eliminate differences."

"The future is battling about limits, regulations, controls where the applications are about making better babies. I don't mind things that add capacities, but I don't like things that narrow choices," he says.

Well, just who is going to legislate these decisions, I ask. I am distressed by this future Reproductive Utopia he is laying out for me.

"I don't know," Caplan says. "Business probably. We do a bad job. The infertility field has no regulation at this point. None. I am talking about who uses it: single moms, older moms, lesbians, drunks, mental defectives. Each center sets its own rules. There are no policies about . . . the egg donor business. If I want to sell an Ivy League egg I can get more money for it . . . the best way to evaluate colleges is the price of their eggs. Princeton wins *(Princeton Mom, did you hear that?)*, Harvard follows. There is a big market in Atlanta. Most of them are coming out of Emory. Japanese people come here for Asian donor eggs because it is not culturally acceptable there."

There are a myriad of other issues that go beyond the making of the baby itself. "We are going to be faced with another weird problem," Caplan says. "Can I be reproduced without permission? More people make embryos. They get divorced. They die. They want to pass them on. Who has the right to control the fate of the embryo? Across generations, can I use them after everyone is dead? Can I will them to my daughter or cousin?"

At this point my head is spinning. I know our conversation has drifted far afield from helping women who are past their prime fertile years have babies, but the implications for the technology are mind-boggling. And this is where it all comes back full circle to the Women's Movement.

"I think something else is going to happen," says Caplan. "Neonatal unity: one giant artificial womb. What will be the limit on prematurity? The 23-24 week limit is about being able to breathe, but someone will come up with something that is analogous to a woman's amniotic fluid . . . [so that] early babies can live. At some point in vitro fertilization meets the fertility clinic, creating babies scientifically in machines."

If—or when—this happens, it will be the great equalizer between men and women, as pregnancy and birth will be taken out of the equation. If gestation occurs outside the mother's womb, both parents are free to work, and drink and eat as much bad food as they want without it affecting the outcome of the pregnancy. Coupled with substantial changes in childcare, having a baby will become a fully equal opportunity endeavor.

"You will see the rise of a big movement to make better babies through chemistry," Caplan says. "Another future fight will be *how* to make a baby. It will replace the abortion debate. 'We can give you the best baby, we can screen your genes, or if you don't like them, we can give you some better genes and grow the baby outside your body and protect it from everything bad'. . . male/female differences we like might be eliminated, leading to economic consequences or power differentials. [Then] the equality comes when the baby is constructed outside the womb and the woman is equal in every way to man."

This sounds like science fiction, I say. "Our grandchildren will experience this," he counters. *(Maybe I should rethink my rush to be a grandparent.)*

"You think you know the issues today? There are big issues coming," Caplan declares. "There will be lots of bioethics work [to come] . . . they now are starting to screen pregnant women and get DNA from the fetus, from the bloodstream. Everybody will routinely screen for everything. It will rapidly move into the standard of care. Lawyers will ask 'why didn't you screen?' Within three years, every birth will have genetic screening."

He goes on to explain the concept of Negative Eugenics, which involves eliminating major problems before they happen. If they are detectable, they can be eliminated from the population.

But what about religion, I ask, thinking of the decline in religious observance cited by Father Jim and Ariela Keysar. What is the moral position here? Can there even *be* a moral ruling for a possibility that was unimaginable when the Bible was written?

"They will say 'we want better babies regardless.' . . . it undermines religion and [the idea] that children with disabilities are gifts from God, accept whatever you get. Now we don't accept and now they are products. We make them. Some of the religious traditions will say [there is] value in all God's children. They are accepting of many different types of people. [But] many parts of the world that are not religious, they will say 'we want better babies.' The ethic of 'Be the Best' will be the underlying ethic. You can tamp it down . . . but we need to put in some protection for disability now."

He sees big class divisions coming, both physically and mentally, between the gifted and not-so-gifted and he cautions that "some of what we value: art, music, theater, poetry" will be lost when eliminating some of these traits. "Here's a good moral question: is it worth having a poet when those people are inclined to depression or mania? It makes for a duller society. It makes for a homogenized society."

His view is broad, long-sighted and visionary. "As medicine extended the life span, we had to create things like recreation, retirement and leisure retirement. We invented leisure; these are not concepts known to Romans or Egyptians. They didn't have hobbies . . . there will be tension between young and old! As we work later and the grandchildren come later, you are starting to compete with your daughter for the same job. [Each generation] wants their shot at the work place."

By this point, I am so *fatootzed* (Urban Dictionary: driven to distraction, derived from Yiddish) I can barely listen. It is all so overwhelming. Think: *Gattaca* (the 1997 movie). Think: Aldous Huxley's *Brave New World*, published in 1932, where natural reproduction has been eliminated and children are created in the laboratory, "decanted" and raised in hatcheries and "conditioning centers." I tell Caplan that he is scaring the urge to grandparent right out of me. He smiles solicitously.

"The job of bioethicist is to alert people to these possibilities—to be prophetic. You better beware. The best the ethicists can do is warn and alert and suggest . . . I still believe the world will be sorted out more by business and commercial forces than by deliberative politics, but I would love to be shown wrong. I have written some of what I am telling you ten years ago, twenty years ago. Politics lags behind, not ethics.

The future will have less disease, less poverty. More money for things other than the healthcare system would be nice. On the other hand, 'Designer Babies' may take issue with what they did get, frustrated that they were given certain skills and begrudge their parents that they didn't get others."

I wonder out loud if my great-grandchild might sue his parents for opting for musical aptitude instead of a great layup shot? Could there be litigation over the choice of traits? Caplan smiles broadly.

"It will be the subject of comedy. It's their world and they will begin to adapt into it." I tell him I am not really sure I want to be around for this brave new world. "We live within our time," he says. "It may be hard to live beyond."

I just want to work on this *next* generation. That would be enough for me.

TWENTY-FOUR

Moving Forward

I have learned a lot through my research. I am not a sociologist or a psychologist or a therapist. What I am is a mother who is looking for answers. Does it help that I am a writer? Sure. That I am curious and persistent? Yup. That I like to talk to people and find out who they are and what they think? Of course. But in the end, I am just a somewhat traditional ol' gal who wants some traditional things: I want to see my daughter have a significant other before I leave this earth so I might go more easily knowing someone loves her like her mama and . . . OH, YES! To hold a grandchild before someone is changing *my* diapers. Two simple goals that are not simple at all, that are no longer even expected societal outcomes.

The marriage rate is down. The birth rate is down. More people than ever are choosing to live alone. The most recent report from *The New York Times* has divorce at an all time low. Claire Cain Miller wrote in an article published December 2, 2014 :

> It is no longer true that the divorce rate is rising, or that half of all marriages end in divorce . . . about 70 percent of marriages that began in the 1990s reached their 15th anniversary (excluding those in which a spouse died), up from about 65 percent of those that

> began in the 1970s and 1980s. Those who married in the 2000s are so far divorcing at even lower rates. If current trends continue, nearly two-thirds of marriages will never involve a divorce.

Well, that's good news.

And there is other good news. An article in *More Magazine* reported a new option for the infertile: embryo adoption. "After embryo cryopreservation was developed more than three decades ago, fertility specialists started routinely freezing extra embryos," writes Sarah Elizabeth Richards in the November 2014 issue. "What happens if [a couple's] desire to have more children runs out before their frozen embryo supply does?"

The options give rise to all kinds of social, emotional and moral questions. The couple can continue to store them for a fee, "donate them for stem cell research . . . or have them thawed and discarded," reports Richards. "The last option is to participate in a growing trend of donating the extra embryos to the one in six couples in the U.S. who have problems conceiving."

So many options. Delay marriage. Delay childbirth. Have a child alone or with the help of someone else's embryo. Dr. Pascale, who you met earlier in her office in New Jersey, worries about this multitude of choices. "We are dangling this stuff in front of people. Our science is providing this opportunity . . . we have created a system where people get what they want so what is the value of 'by chance'? The ability to modify genes and sex is here to stay. They are not going to have any surprises. This is the price we are paying for choice and information. And I think it is going to be a big price."

Forget about having kids. How about coupling at all? Dr. Diller says she tells her clients "they are part of a generation of men and women who are not marrying so much. They seem less interested in their twenties, thirties, forties." She cites "the cost of raising a child" as a large factor.

Dr. Nachtigall is on board with that. "Our whole economy, the metropolitan centers in particular . . . none of us could stay in Manhattan without two incomes and give kids what they need. The two-income family for middle class and above is necessary . . . the system has changed."

It is a hard reality for the young woman who comes to the city to fulfill her career aspirations, meet a mate and have a family. She is supposed to be most productive at work at the same time her ovaries are most productive, while looking for a husband as the pool of eligible candidates (both men and eggs) dwindles with each passing year. The dilemma has not changed much for women, despite their freedom to work as hard as men. They are still expected to choose or miss the opportunity, in both arenas. And if you do try and have it all, and you are lucky enough to find someone to share the journey with, you have to make some spectacular money to fund it. We can't all be CEOs with helpful husbands.

But what if the dream doesn't materialize? What if Prince Charming doesn't appear in time to capitalize on your fertility? There is still a good life to be made. There is growing acceptance of alternative paths to a family as well as those who opt to skip it all and move on, building a different kind of life altogether, a happy life with neo-kin.

I think of the guests at a contemporary metropolitan holiday table, the relations you choose and those that come with the meal. Look around: there is your single daughter and her gay friend who brings his lover with whom he is adopting the baby that their surrogate is carrying. All three are present with casseroles of quinoa and kale, as is the newly engaged couple (heterosexual) and the newly marrieds (homosexual) and your husband's old roommate who is going through transition, awaiting sex reassignment surgery. Here is the sister you are talking to at the moment with the grandson she is caring for while his parents are deployed. There is grandma and her new boyfriend, your yoga teacher and her nephew who is estranged from his parents and is hitting on your daughter. Also your old boss, divorced cousin and her loud-mouthed neighbor, Lou.

It's a mixed-up group of people reflecting many lifestyles. Unconventional by yesterday's standards, yes, but not by today's. It is a family by choice and proximity, if not by birth, and often defined by the variety of backgrounds and experience its members bring. It is most definitely not our mother's table.

Betty Friedan wrote:

> In my generation, many of us knew that we did not want to be like our mothers, even when we loved them. We could not help but see their disappointment. Did we understand, or only resent, the sadness, the emptiness, that made them hold too fast to us, try to live our lives, run our fathers' lives, spend their days . . . yearning for things that never satisfied them. Strangely, many others who loved their daughters—and mine was one—did not want their daughters to grow up like them either. They knew we needed something more.

"The Women's Movement never promised that life wouldn't be a struggle," writes Leslie Bennets. "[It] never promised that it would be easy to combine meaningful work with raising a family—only that it should be possible."

But I don't think the women who wrote the manifesto ever anticipated that we would raise our daughters to be so empowered by choice, that in the choosing of career they might miss their chance for children altogether. They may cobble together satisfactory new families and/or devote themselves to high-powered achievements in the marketplace, but it does not alter the fact that they have missed out on a basic part of womanhood. Some will be fine with this. Others will not. Those are the women I have written this book for. Them, and their mothers.

You might notice that I have not included Gloria Steinem in this work. I haven't quoted her or cited her writing and I have given this much thought. How could I not include her in this conversation? It's taken me the whole process of writing this book to understand it myself. Having grown up with a mother who suffered from mental illness, she is not unlike me. Yet we are worlds apart. She learned early that it was important to be self-sufficient, to be able to make her own way. She fought hard, built a movement, and changed a generation of minds. But where Gloria was militant, I was needy. Where she was beautiful, tall, sexy, I was not. Many men wanted her—either to possess her or take her down. She made me feel inadequate in both my appearance and my politics. There was no way I could be out there burning my bra. I was big-busted and needed support. Lots of support. In so many ways.

Betty was my gal. She was a short, stocky Jewish lady. She

had been there and done that. The whole housewife/motherhood *magillah*. She was the mother of the movement for me, where Gloria was the maiden aunt. Are the women I am writing about now the daughters she never had? In the end, are they Gloria's Girls? She may be proud of their achievements and equality, but how does it feel at the end of the day? These are the daughters of her intellect and initiative, but not her womb. They are accomplished but barren. And they have remained so because of her valiant fight for their reproductive freedom.

Bennets says:

> Although the concept of choice was indeed a hallmark of the Women's Movement, many of the toughest challenges faced by women today are not our choice at all; they have been imposed on us by a larger society that continues to shortchange the needs of women and children. These problems can be addressed only with individual and collective action.

This should be a clear and conscious call to Sheryl Sandberg and the other pundits currently addressing women's issues today. It is time for them to carry forth the banner that Freidan and Steinem painted. It is much more complicated than leaning in to a career and establishing a foundation. It is not enough to skate through the talk show circuit and tweet the talk. To make change there must be new legislation. We need to learn from countries like Sweden. Affordable childcare and health services need to be in place for any woman who wants to bear a child, regardless of her marital status. And yes, Sheryl, parking places for the pregnant. Have you ever thought about running for office, Ms. Sandberg? I would be happy to bake cookies for the volunteers. You know, that old tee-shirt slogan is still applicable: A Woman's Place is in the House . . . and Senate.

But why not you, my youngest son asks. Why don't YOU get political? It is a valid question and my own personal fatal flaw is embedded in the answer. This is about as political as I get. I am limited. My desire for change is overridden by my desire for the traditional; I have never let go of my own warped desire for Happily Ever After. Instead, I have put my faith in this next generation. They are the movers and shakers. They will be the makers of change.

As I am trying to bring this book to a meaningful conclusion, I reach out to women of my generation who have had high-powered careers and ask them how they were empowered to choose career over family at a time when I did not even know I had a choice. We were on the cusp of a movement and they rode the wave while I stayed on shore.

I am surprised by the answer. Many say their parents—mostly their fathers—encouraged them to have a profession so they would never be dependent on a man financially. It is just as important, if not more so, today.

In retrospect, I think my own father never even thought those thoughts. He and my mother were too entrenched in their own battle for survival to worry about mine. This is one of the things I have learned in middle age: they did the best they could. I thank them now for directing me towards teaching. I have "fallen back" on it many, many times. It hasn't been lucrative for me, but it has provided a flexible—and often fun—way for me to work part-time and be available to my children full-time. It has given me the freedom to write. I have had a substantial helping of both worlds, if not a full meal.

I thought by the time I got here, I would have found a satisfactory answer to why these women have missed their boat. I have not. I am left with a bitter taste, some self-recriminations and a residue of sadness that I cannot kick. If we are not actually to blame, we are still responsible for those daughters who thought "Happily Ever After" would just happen to them. Perhaps the portion of blame that falls to us lies in our need and desire to protect them from all of life's disappointments. But now, their disappointment is our disappointment as they move forward without spouses or children.

"Perhaps younger women don't understand the appeal of combining work and family because we failed to tell them how great it can be," Bennets writes. "Did we somehow forget to express our delight in those rewards? Have we failed to articulate the deep satisfaction of building independent lives and enjoying professional success as well as loving families?"

It is our obligation to support our young women as they forge different kinds of families, to treat them with dignity and lift the shame of being unpregnant or unmarried. It is essential to welcome them to the adult table and offer them a room of their own. It is important for them to know that they, by themselves, are enough. We must grieve the dream with them and then stop grieving and create a new "Happily Ever After." Even if it's furry and has four paws. We must embrace what is.

EPILOGUE

It is Thursday morning. The phone rings at 2 AM. It can only be one thing: the baby. My daughter-in-law's water has broken. They are well trained in a popular childbirth method, she and my son, and have been advised to wait at home for contractions to begin. The call is strictly informational. "Stay," my son says. "I will keep you posted." We stay.

I shower and wash my hair. No call. I blow it dry. Nothing. We turn on the television and watch the *Way Too Early* show. We are too revved up to sleep. Streaks of light begin to stripe the dark waters of the Hudson River, separating us from our children in New York City.

It is full out dawn and we have not been called. Can we text? I ask my husband? He shrugs, noncommittal.

"Should we come?" I type.

"No," my son answers.

By late morning, we are dozing off. My husband elects not to go to work as he thinks we will be leaving for the hospital soon. The phone rings. My son reports they have been told to wait at home for contractions to begin. Their childbirth instructor advises waiting 24 hours after the water has broken before heading in.

The day drags on. He calls again to say they are going to the hospital. Stay home, he says. There are no contractions.

We get dinner. The sun sets. The buildings across the river glow pink in its reflection. We watch a lot of stupid television and wait. And wait. We try to sleep and another night goes by.

My son and his wife are not ready for a caesarian section yet. Neither is the baby. There is a good strong heartbeat. The doctors are okay with letting my daughter-in-law wait for labor to begin. In the morning of the second day, they agree to induce. They try a natural approach. It doesn't work. They wait. We wait.

The doctor starts Pitocin and she moves from one to two centimeters. Nothing more. Our son texts us an update every few hours to say that there is nothing new to say. My husband forbids me to call. It is nightfall. We eat again, I think.

I put on pajamas, but lay my clothes out just in case we get another middle of the night call. It has been 48 hours. Fear sets in. This isn't right. It is too long.

You can*not* call him, my husband says. You *must* wait.

Even if it is bad news. You must wait. I begin to cry big, silent tears.

My son is my bonus baby. My obstetrician called him that when he told me I was pregnant again after losing Jillian. "This one's on the house," he said. "I promise. I will deliver a healthy baby for you." History should not repeat itself.

I think back. I am two weeks before my due date and a stress test detects fetal distress. I am admitted to the hospital and they attach me to monitors. They watch. I tremble. The baby's heart beat dips down. They watch. It dips again and again. I am rushed to delivery. They administer the epidural and I feel them reach inside me and pull my son from my womb. The umbilical cord is wrapped around his arm and his thigh several times. They untangle him, swab him, swaddle him. He is pink and wailing. I cry with relief.

His baby must be okay. I am paralyzed by fear. I wait. I do not sleep.

50 hours have passed. "This is too long," I say.

"Shhhh," says my husband. He is too fearful to talk.

51 hours. This can't be right. Something must be terribly wrong. They have assured me many times that cord problems are not hereditary, and certainly not from mother to daughter-in-law.

52 hours.

53. The phone rings. It is my son.

The excruciating waiting is finally over.

We have a beautiful, healthy grandson.

Let the grandparenting begin.

ABOUT THE AUTHOR

Debbie Slevin

Debbie Slevin is a writer, producer/director and teacher. After 25 years of nurturing the theatrical yearnings of countless students, she decided to devote her creative energy to exploring her own artistic capabilities.

Theatrical accomplishments include *The Apron Strings Project* in Riverhead, NY, which she conceived and co-produced, *The Last Five Years*, which she produced and directed in East Hampton, NY and the first NYC revival of *Songs for a New World*. Her original play *Gate B23: Carry-On Baggage* was a selection of Manhattan Repertory Theater's Winterfest and the International Fringe Festival held in NYC.

A regular contributor to the Hamptons' *Dan's Papers*, Debbie's writing has appeared in magazines and newspapers including *Essence*, *Woman's World*, *Lifestyles*, *Reform Judaism* and *The Record*. She was a staff writer for *The Jewish Standard* and a columnist for *DogWatch*, a newsletter of Cornell University's School of Veterinary Medicine.

UnPregnant Pause: Where Are the Babies? is Debbie's first published title. Her essay "Beach Art" was the winning selection of Word Up: Long Island LitFest. She also has written two novels, *A Good Man* and *The Hitting Chair*, and has just completed a new play about Mark Twain's women.

Debbie is married with three children and one grandchild.

ACKNOWLEDGEMENTS

There are many people who helped make this book possible. I am so grateful to all of you.

I met my publisher Sandy Ghattas-Akseizer at a women's networking event at my husband's office where a casual conversation took a fateful turn. Thank you, Certified Financial Services, for creating this welcoming environment. Thank you, Sandy, for your encouragement, support and dedication to the details and also to Matthew John Hadodo for your concise and careful editing. You both put a tremendous amount of yourselves into this project, and I am so appreciative.

Candice DiLavore is the best researcher a writer could hope for. Your many hours of diligent attention to specifics and your sharp, probing mind helped me become a better writer. You are a talented woman with an astute perspective and I look forward to reading your book someday.

My dear friend and kindred spirit Nancy Amsel gave me the most important element of this book: a personal introduction to the best of the best working in fertility medicine. Those interviews took this book from a wannabe grandma's lament into a fully researched exploration of an issue. I am forever indebted to you. I graciously thank all the professionals who took time out of their busy schedules to meet with me and answer my emails. You are the bones of the book. The chapters in which you are featured give structure and veracity to this endeavor. A special "shout-out" to Father James DiLuzio for your friendship and heartfelt spiritual conversations and to Sister Eileen Clifford of the Archdiocese of New York for providing me with research material.

The flesh of the book grows from the women who must remain unnamed. You've shared your stories, often through your tears. You've been so open, generous and raw with me, and I don't know how I could ever thank you enough for letting me into your lives. I deeply wish for you that which you wish for yourselves. Thank you especially to my dear friend from the Arkham days. Your courage, intellect and deep humanity continue to inspire me. In many ways, I wrote this book because of you.

The heart of the book belongs to the women in my life, starting with my book club: Melinda Iannuzzi, Jan Miller, Susan Sunshine, Elaine Kass, AnnaMaria Porto, Viviene Lampach and Jackie Lustgarten. You have spoken openly and at great length with me about this subject over many delicious meals in each other's homes. You have challenged me and been my cheerleaders. Your presence has given me a wealth of love, support, humor, encouragement and friendship for many years. I want to thank Connie Heymann for almost 55 years of friendship, Anita Katz for 40 years of "being there," Judith Brown for being a terrific listener through all those lunches since Euclid Avenue and Leslie Schlesinger, who has just the best ideas. I also want to thank Leslie Pearlman of Good Ground Yoga who has taught me how to breathe and how to let it go.

The soul of my writing is my family. Thank you to my daughter Bailie, who has graciously gone on record herein, and my daughter-in-law Marlo, who has allowed me to use details of her life. My new daughter-in-law Kirstin provided invaluable marketing advice and my sons Ted and Mickey utilized their protective instincts and astute business acumen to guide me through the more practical aspects of this process. Thank you to my brother Jerry for providing more than enough unconditional support to make up for all our childhood dysfunction, and of course, my husband Jeff, who in addition to his love and support, has provided me with financial freedom to pursue my art. Whenever I wonder if I should have been home less and out more trying to build a bigger career, I look at all of you and I am convinced that you are my best, my most cherished life's work. And then I am at peace with my decision.

NOTES

TWO: THE READING ROOM

1. Sandberg, S. (2014). *Lean in: Women, Work and the Will to Lead.* Random House.
2. Patton, S. (2014). *Marry Smart, Advice for Finding "The One"* Gallery Books, Simon & Shuster.
3. Bennets, L. (2007).*The Feminine Mistake.* Hyperion, 35-36
4. Idem,153
5. Patton, S.193
6. Sandberg, S. 24
7. Patton, S. xvii
8. Idem. 8
9. Fels, A. (2004) *Necessary Dreams, Ambition in Woman's Changing Lives Pantheon*, xvi
10. Greer, G. (1970) *The Female Eunuch* McGraw-Hill, 88
11. Friedan, B. (1997) *The Feminine Mystique*, WW Norton, 75
12. Bennets, L. 152

THREE: IT'S BIOLOGY BABY: THE BIG KAHUNA

1. Erikson, E. (1959) Identity and the Life Cycle, W. H. Norton
2. http://grandparenting.org/resource/making-of-a-grandparent/
3. http://www.nyufertilitycenter.org/egg_freezing/success_rates

FOUR: IT'S BIOLOGY BABY: THE PRAGMATIC PATHOLOGIST

1. Whereas all of my other experts gave permission to use their given names, he and his university have requested that I not use his real name or title. I have also changed the names of his family members.

FIVE: IT'S BIOLOGY, MAMA: DON'T WASTE TIME!

1. *New York Times* "Vows" section, September 7, 14, 21, 2014

SIX: BY THE NUMBERS

1. http://www.infoplease.com/ipa/A0005061
2. http://www.cdc.gov/nchs/data/databriefs/db21.pdf
3. CDC/ NCHS Data Brief, no. 21. August 2009 National Vital Statistics System
4. http://www.cdc.gov/nchs/data/databriefs/db21.pdf

EIGHT: BACK TO SCHOOL

1. http://nwsa.org/projects/database/index.php
2. http://bitchmagazine.org/article/everything-about-feminism-you-wanted-to-know-but-were-afraid-to-ask
3. http://mdbrady.wordpress.com/2012/04/07/of-woman-born-motherhood-as-experience-and-institution-by-adrienne-rich/
4. http://entertainment.time.com/2014/01/31/theres-now-a-college-course-about-beyonce-at-rutgers-university/.Rutgers University offers new course: "Politicizing Beyonce" in the Department of Women's and Gender Studies. The class will use the performer's music and career to explore race, gender and sexual politics in modern America.

TEN: HOW'S YOUR DADDY?

1. Meeker, M. (2006). Strong Fathers, Strong Daughters, Regnery Pub, 8
2. Idem 232-5

ELEVEN: LETS HEAR IT FROM THE MEN

1. Kimmel, M. (2008). *Guyland: The Perilous World Where Boys become Men.* Harper Collins, 38
2. Dowd, M. (2005) *Are Men Necessary*, Putnam Books, 47
3. Idem. 106
4. Kimmel, 251
5. Dowd, 138

TWELVE: FIRST COMES LOVE, THEN COMES MARRIAGE?

1. http://www.cnn.com/2014/10/15/opinion/schwartz-single-women/
2. http://www.census.gov/prod/2011pubs/11statab/vitstat.pdf
3. "The Changing American Family" Nov. 25, 2013 *The New York Times*
4. Bogel, K. (2008). *Hooking Up: Sex, Dating, and Relationships on Campus*, New York University Press, 76
5. Idem, 38
6. Freitas, D. (2013) *The End of Sex: How Hookup Culture Is Leaving a Generation Unhappy, Sexually Unfulfilled, and Confused About Intimacy*, Basic Books, 182
7. Bolick, K. (2011) http://www.theatlantic.com/magazine/archive/2011/11/all-the-single-ladies/308654/

THIRTEEN: TEA AND DEMOGRAPHICS

1. Keysar, A. (2014) National Demographic Survey of American Jewish College Students. http://www.trincoll.edu/Academics/centers/isssc/Documents/HighlightJewishCollegeStudentSurvey.pdf
2. A kibbutz is a small, self-supporting community within Israel.

FOURTEEN: COURAGE TO GO IT ALONE

1. Mattes, J. (1997) *Single Mothers by Choice, Three Rivers* Press, xix
2. Ibid.
3. Idem, 12-3
4. Idem, 17
5. Idem, 21
6. Idem, 125

SEVENTEEN: DIVORCE AND DAMAGE

1. http://www.census.gov/prod/2011pubs/11statab/vitstat.pdf
2. Greer, G. (1970). *The Female Eunuch*, McGraw Hill, 12

TWENTY: IT'S BIOLOGY . . . OR IT ISN'T

1. Annis, B. (2010) *Same Words Different Language*, Piatkus Publishers, 30

2. Idem, 32
3. Barnett, R and Rivers, C. (2004). *Same Difference*, Basic Books, 6
4. Idem, 13
5. Idem, 224
6. http://www.singlesexschools.org/research-learning.htm
7. 2002 "Making the grade but feeling distressed: gender differences in academic performance and internal distress," Journal of Educational Psychology, vol. 94, 2, 396-404
8. Orenstein, P. (2011). *Cinderella Ate my Daughter*, Harper Collins, 5
9. Idem, 34
10. Idem, 38
11. Idem, 49-50
12. Orenstein, 137-8
13. Idem, 101

TWENTY-ONE: HIP TO BE SINGLE

1. Rosenbloom, S. (2014) *Zeroing In on the Female Traveler The Getaway*, New York Times, August 3
2. Klinenberg, E. (2012). *Going Solo, The Extraordinary Rise and Surprising Appeal of Living Alone*, Penguin Press, 5
3. Idem, 13
4. Idem, 14-5
5. Idem, 25-6
6. Idem, 30
7. Idem, 59
8. Kaufman, J. (2014) "The Buddy System" *The New York Times*, Real Estate Section, August 17
9. Ibid
10. Klinenberg, 185
11. Idem, 203
12. Idem, 207
13. Idem, 222
14. Ibid

TWENTY-TWO: WHAT'S NEXT?

1. Magnus, G. (2009). *The Age of Aging* John Wiley & Sons, 4
2. Idem, 18
3. Diller, V. (2010). *Psychology Today*, May 29

REFERENCES

Angier, N. (2013, November 25). The Changing American Family. *The New York Times.* Retrieved from http://www.nytimes.com/2013/11/26/health/families.html?pagewanted=all

Annis, B. (2010). *Same Words, Different Language.* US: Barbara Annis and Associates.

Barnett, R. C., & Rivers, C. (2004). *Same Difference: How Gender Myths Are Hurting Our Relationships, Our Children, and Our Jobs.* New York: Basic Books.

Bennetts, L. (2007). *The Feminine Mistake: Are We Giving Up Too Much?* New York: Hyperion.

Bessette, C. (2014, October 14). Apple, Facebook to Women Employees: Keep Working, We'll Pay to Freeze Your Eggs. Forbes. Retrieved from http://www.forbes.com/sites/chanellebessette/2014/10/14/apple-facebook-to-female-employees-keep-working-well-pay-to-freeze-your-eggs/

Bloomberg, M., & Burden, A. (2006, December). New York City population projections by age/sex & borough 2000-2030. *Department of City Planning.* Retrieved from http://www.nyc.gov/html/dcp/pdf/census/projections_briefing_booklet.pdf

Bogel, K. A. (2008). *Hooking Up: Sex, Dating, and Relationships on Campus.* New York: New York University Press.

Bolick, K. (2011, November). All the single ladies. *The Atlantic.* Retrieved from http://www.theatlantic.com/magazine/archive/2011/11/all-the-single-ladies/308654/

Boston Women's Health Book Collective. (2009). *Our Bodies, Ourselves.* New York: Touchstone.

Brady, M.D. (2012, April 7). Of Woman Born: Motherhood As Experience and Institution, by Adrienne Rich [Review of the book: *Of Woman Born: Motherhood As Experience and Institution*]. Retrieved from Me, You, and Books website: https://mdbrady.wordpress.com/2012/04/07/of-woman-born-motherhood-as-experience-and-institution-by-adrienne-rich/

Centers for Disease Control and Prevention. (2015, February 19). National marriage and divorce rate trends. *National Vital Statistics System.* Retrieved from http://www.cdc.gov/nchs/nvss/marriage_divorce_tables.htm

Centers for Disease Control and Prevention. (2011). Divorce rates by state: 1990, 1995, and 1999-2011. Retrieved from http://www.cdc.gov/nchs/data/dvs/divorce_rates_90_95_99-11.pdf

Clinton, H. R. (1995). *It Takes a Village: And Other Lessons Children Teach Us.* New York, NY: Simon & Schuster.

Cobble, D., Gordon, L., & Henry, A. (2014). *Feminism Unfinished, A Short History of the Women's Movements.* New York: WW Norton & Co.

Collins, G. (2009). *When Everything Changed: The Amazing Journey of American Women from 1960 to the Present.* New York: Little, Brown & Co.

Cohen, S., Ukeles, J., & Miller, R. (June 2012). Jewish Community Study of New York: 2011 Comprehensive Report. *UJA-Federation of New York.* Retrieved from http://www.jewishdatabank.org/Studies/downloadFile.cfm?FileID=2852

Copen, C., Daniels, K., Vespa, J., & Mosher, W. (March 22, 2012). First Marriages in the United States: Data From the 2006-2010 National Survey of Family Growth. *National Center for Health Statistics*. (National Health Statistics Reports no 49). Retrieved from http://www.cdc.gov/nchs/data/nhsr/nhsr049.pdf

Coontz, S. (2011). A Strange Stirring, *The Feminine Mystique and American Women at the Dawn of the 1960s*. Philadelphia: Basic Books.

Curtin, S., Ventura, S., & Martinez, G. (August 2014). Declines in non-marital childbearing in the United States. *National Center for Health Statistics*. (NCHS Data Brief No. 162). Retrieved from http://www.cdc.gov/nchs/data/databriefs/db162.pdf

Davies, C., & Williams, D. (May 2002). The Grandparent Study 2002 Report. *AARP*. Retrieved from http://assets.aarp.org/rgcenter/general/gp_2002.pdf

De Beauvoir, S. (1949). *The Second Sex*. (Borde, C., & Malovany-Chevalier, S., Trans.) New York: Knopf.

Diller, V. (2012, May 21). Are you a 'new' (as opposed to 'old') grand-parent? *Huffington Post*. Retrieved from http://www.huffingtonpost.com/vivian-diller-phd/the-new-as-opposed-to-old_b_1529428.html

Dockterman, E. (2014, January 31). There's now a college course about Beyonce at Rutgers University. *Time*. Retrieved from http://entertainment.time.com/2014/01/31/theres-now-a-college-course-about-beyonce-at-rut-gers-university/

Dowd, M. (2005). *Are Men Necessary?: When Sexes Collide*. New York: Putnam Publishing Group.

Edelman, S. (2013, June 2). Ova easy: Egg-freeze calculator. *NY Post*.

Retrieved from http://nypost.com/2013/06/02/ova-easy-egg-freeze-calculator/

Erikson, E. (1967). *Identity and the Life Cycle.* New York: W.W. Norton & Company.

Fels, A. (2004). *Necessary Dreams: Ambition in Women's Changing Lives.* New York: Random House.

Fey, T. (2011). *Bossypants.* New York: Little, Brown & Company.

Field, A. (2014, October 5). A Hands-On Toy Teaching Girls to Lean In. *Forbes.* Retrieved from http://www.forbes.com/sites/annefield/2014/10/05/a-hands-on-toy-teaching-girls-to-lean-in/

Freidan, B. (1963). *The Feminine Mystique.* New York: W.W. Norton & Company.

Freitas, D. (2013). *The End of Sex: How Hookup Culture is Leaving a Generation Unhappy, Sexually Unfulfilled, and Confused About Intimacy.* New York: Basic Books.

Fudge, R. (2005). Everything you always wanted to know about feminism but were afraid to ask. *Bitch Media.* Retrieved from http://bitchmagazine.org/article/everything-about-feminism-you-wanted-to-know-but-were-afraid-to-ask

Greer, G. (1970). *The Female Eunuch.* New York: Farrar Straus Giroux.

Heilburn, C. (1995). *Education of a Woman: The Life of Gloria Steinem.* New York: Ballentine.

Isen, A., & Stevenson, B. (2010, February). Women's Education and Family Behavior: Trends in Marriage, Divorce and Fertility. *National Bureau of*

Economic Research. Retrieved from http://www.nber.org/papers/w15725.pdf?new_window=1

Livingston, G., & Brown, A. (2014, August 13). Birthrate for unmarried women declining for the first time in decades. *Pew Research Center*. Retrieved from http://www.pewresearch.org/fact-tank/2014/08/13/birth-rate-for-unmarried-women-declining-for-first-time-in-decades/

Keysar A., & Kosmin, B. A. (2014). Demographic survey of American Jewish college students 2014. *Trinity College*. Retrieved from http://www.trincoll.edu/Academics/centers/isssc/Documents/HighlightJewishCollegeStudentSurvey.pdf

Keysar, A., & Kosmin, B.A. (2009). *Secularism, Women, & The State: The Mediterranean World in the 21st Century*. Hartford: Institute for the Study of Secularism in Sociey and Culture, Trinity College.

Kaufman, J. (2014, August 15). The buddy system: Sharing a New York apartment by choice. *The New York Times*. Retrieved from http://www.nytimes.com/2014/08/17/realestate/sharing-a-new-york-apartment-by-choice.html

Kilenberg, E. (2012). *Going Solo: The Extraordinary Rise and Surprising Appeal of Living Alone*. New York: The Penguin Press HC.

Kimmel, M. (2008). *Guyland: The Perilous World Where Boys Become Men*. New York: HarperCollins Publishers.

Magnus, G. (2009). *The Age of Aging*. Singapore: John Wiley & Sons.

Martin, J., Hamilton, B., Osterman, M., Curtin, S., & Matthews, T.J. (2013, December 20). Births: Final Data for 2012. *National Vital Statistics Reports*, 62(9). Retrieved from http://www.cdc.gov/nchs/data/nvsr/nvsr62/nvsr62_09.pdf#table

Mattes, J. (1994). *Single Mothers by Choice: A Guidebook for Single Women Who Are Considering or Have Chosen Motherhood.* New York: Three Rivers Press.

Matthews, T.J., & Hamilton B. (2009, August). Delayed childbearing: More women are having their first child later in life. *Centers for Disease Control and Prevention.* (NCHS Data Brief No. 21). Retrieved from http://www.cdc.gov/nchs/data/databriefs/db21.pdf

Meeker, M. (2006). *Strong Fathers, Strong Daughters: 10 Secrets Every Father Should Know.* Washington, DC: Regnery Publishing.

Miller, C.C. (2014, December 2). The divorce surge is over, but the myth lives on. *The New York Times.* Retrieved from http://www.nytimes.com/2014/12/02/upshot/the-divorce-surge-is-over-but-the-myth-lives-on.html?abt=0002&abg=1

Notkin, M. (2014). *Otherhood: Modern Women Finding A New Kind of Happiness.* New York: Seal Press.

Orenstein, P. (2011). *Cinderella Ate My Daughter.* New York: HarperCollins Publishers.

Patton, S. (2014). *Marry Smart: Advice for Finding THE ONE.* New York: Gallery Books.

Peters, J. (2001). *Not Your Mother's Life, Changing Rules of Work, Love and Family.* Philadelphia: Perseus Publishing.

Pomerantz, A., Altermatt, E., & Saxon, J. (2002). Making the grade but feeling distressed: gender differences in academic performance and internal distress. *Journal of Educational Psychology*, 94, (2), 396-404. Retrieved from http://psycnet.apa.org/psycinfo/2002-13338-014

Ratner, A. (2014, October 13). The boardroom and the bedroom. Slate. Retrieved from http://www.slate.com/articles/technology/future_tense/2014/10/how_both_dating_and_finance_have_been_screwed_by_the_internet.2.html

Reynolds, M., Shagle, S., & Venkatarman, L. (2007, December 26). A national census of women's and gender studies programs in U.S. institutions of higher education. *National Opinion Research Center.* Retrieved from http://www.nwsa.org/files/NWSA_CensusonWSProgs.pdf

Rhodes, G. and Stanley, S. (2014). Before "I Do," What do premarital experiences have to do with marital quality among today's young adults? *The National Marriage Project at the University of Virginia.* Retrieved from http://nationalmarriageproject.org/wp-content/uploads/2014/08/NMP-BeforeIDoReport-Final.pdf

Rich, A. (1976). *Of Woman Born: Motherhood as Experience and Institution.* New York: W.W. Norton & Company.

Richards, S.E. (2014, November). Could you give your embryos to a stranger? More. Retrieved from http://www.more.com/news/womens-issues/leftover-ivf-embryo-donation?page=2

Rosenbloom, S. (2014, July 31). Zeroing in on the female traveler. *The New York Times.* Retrieved from http://www.nytimes.com/2014/08/03/travel/zeroing-in-on-the-female-traveler.html

Sandberg, S. (2013). *Lean In: Women, Work, and the Will to Lead.* New York: Knopf.

Sarkeesian, A. (2012, January 30). LEGO Friends – LEGO & Gender Part 1. Retrieved from http://feministfrequency.com/2012/01/30/lego-gender-part-1-lego-friends/

Schulte, B. (2014, September 24). I do? No thanks. The economics of America's marriage decline. *The Washington Post.* Retrieved from http://www.washingtonpost.com/news/storyline/wp/2014/09/24/i-do-no-thanks-the-economics-behind-americas-marriage-decline/

Schwartz, P. (2014, October 15). Why more women choose not to marry. *CNN.* Retrieved from http://www.cnn.com/2014/10/15/opinion/schwartz-single-women/

Shulz, N. (2013). *Home Economics: The Consequences of Changing Family Structure.* Washington, DC: AEI Press.

Sommers, C. H. (2013). *Freedom Feminism.* Washington, DC: AEI Press.

Story, L. (2005, September 20). Many Women at Elite Colleges Set Career Path to Motherhood. *The New York Times.* Retrieved from http://www.nytimes.com/2005/09/20/national/20women.html?pagewanted=1&_r=0

Taylor, K. (2013, July 12). Sex on Campus: She Can Play That Game, Too. *The New York Times.* Retrieved from http://www.nytimes.com/2013/07/14/fashion/sex-on-campus-she-can-play-that-game-too.html?pagewanted=all&_r=1

Tejada-Vera, B., & Sutton, P.D. (2010, August 27). Births, marriages, divorces, and deaths: Provisional data for 2009. *National Vital Statistics Reports,* 58(25). Retrieved from http://www.cdc.gov/nchs/data/nvsr/nvsr58/nvsr58_25.pdf

Toossi, M. (2005, November). Labor force projections to 2014: retiring boomers. *Occupational Statistics and Employment Projections, Bureau of Labor Statistics.* Retrieved from http://www.bls.gov/opub/mlr/2005/11/art3full.pdf

US Census Bureau. (2011). Births, deaths, marriages, and divorces.

Retrieved from http://www.census.gov/prod/2011pubs/11statab/vitstat.pdf

Vaillant, G. E. (2012). *Triumphs of Experience: The Men of the Harvard Grant Study*. Cambridge, Massachusetts: Belknap Press.

Ventura, S., Hamilton, BE., & Matthews, T.J. (2014, August 20). National and State Patterns of Teen Births in the United States, 1940-2013. *National Vital Statistics Reports*, 63(4). Retrieved from http://www.cdc.gov/nchs/data/nvsr/nvsr63/nvsr63_04.pdf

Wang, W., & Parker, K. (2014, September 24). Record Share of American Have Never Married. *Pew Research Center*. Retrieved from http://www.pewsocialtrends.org/2014/09/24/record-share-of-americans-have-never-married/

Wilcox, B. (2014, June 20). Book Review: 'Marriage Markets' by June Carbone and Naomi Cahn [Review of the book *Marriage Markets*]. *The Wall Street Journal.* Retrieved from http://www.wsj.com/articles/book-review-marriage-markets-by-june-carbone-and-naomi-cahn-1403295461?cb=logged0.08684520842507482

CPSIA information can be obtained at www.ICGtesting.com
Printed in the USA
BVOW08s1643031115

425448BV00004B/7/P